HOW TO OPEN AND OPERATE
A HOME-BASED
SECRETARIAL SERVICES BUSINESS

HOW TO OPEN AND OPERATE A HOME-BASED SECRETARIAL SERVICES BUSINESS

by Jan Melnik

OLD SAYBROOK, CONNECTICUT

This book's purpose is to provide accurate and authoritative information on the topics covered. It is sold with the understanding that neither the author nor the publisher is engaged in rendering legal, financial, accounting, or other professional services. Neither the Globe Pequot Press nor the author assumes any liability resulting from action taken based on the information included herein. Mention of a company name does not constitute endorsement.

Copyright © 1994 by Jan Melnik

All rights reserved. No part of this book may be reproduced or transmitted in any form by any means, electronic or mechanical, including photocopying and recording, or by any information storage and retrieval system, except as may be expressly permitted by the 1976 Copyright Act or by the publisher. Requests for permission should be made in writing to The Globe Pequot Press, P.O. Box 833, Old Saybrook, Connecticut 06475.

Cover and text illustrations by Kathy Michalove

Library of Congress Cataloging-in-Publication Data

Melnik, Jan.
  How to open and operate a home-based secretarial services business / by Jan Melnik. — 1st ed.
    p. cm.
  Includes bibliographical references.
  ISBN 1-56440-398-X
  1. Secretaries. 2. Typewriting services. 3. Home-based businesses. I. Title.
HF5547.5.M446 1994
651.3'7'068—dc20   93-42694
              CIP

Manufactured in the United States of America
First Edition/Third Printing

To Danny, Westy, and Stephen, my "honeys" with the great big hugs . . . and Ron, always, for inspiration . . . my love.

Contents

Acknowledgments

My sincere thanks and appreciation to:

Understanding clients, for their support and patience . . .

Julie Lynch, for the right connection . . .

Mike Urban, for the opportunity . . .

Wonderful NASS colleagues and friends, for their enthusiasm for this project and their willingness to share their stories over the years . . .

My editor, Mace Lewis, for his encouragement and expertise as well as providing a wonderful "excuse" (along with Laurie!) to re-live all those incredible "early twin" memories while we worked on this together . . .

Louise McGuire Kursmark, for helping me get my business off the ground in 1983 with her good advice, moral support, and deep friendship—and just always being there . . .

Nana and Grampa, for my entrepreneurial passion . . .

Mom, for insisting that I learn to type . . .

Dad, for my love of reading and my thirst for words . . .

All my "Melnik Men," for their love and support!

Introduction

The beginning is the most important part of the work.

— PLATO, *The Republic*, Book 1 (c. 320 B.C.)

In creating, the only hard thing's to begin;
A grass-blade's no easier to make than an oak.

— JAMES RUSSELL LOWELL, *A Fable for Critics* (1848)

As with so many things in life, particularly those things most worth doing, getting started and actually beginning can sometimes be the most challenging steps.

I always knew I would someday work for myself. For a number of years prior to starting my company, I'd experienced some margin of success as a freelance writer, with my byline appearing in local newspapers and magazines as well as several national publications. But it wasn't until 1982, when my roommate from college and dear friend Louise McGuire Kursmark decided to start *her* own business providing secretarial services, that I began to really contemplate owning my own business.

Lou had her first child in October of that year and determined that the sometimes inevitable return to the "corporate rat race" after her maternity leave ended was not for her. Instead, she started "Secretarial Services Unlimited" from her home (at that time in North Reading, Massachusetts; now, known as "Best Impression," down the road a few miles, in Reading). Because we'd always stayed in close contact, I watched every step of her business growth, and within a few months she was well on her way to success—clientele was becoming established, cash was coming in, it was looking good. I shared her initial excitement and realized the appeal this opportunity offered.

My own circumstances at that time were different from my friend's. I was on a "career fast track" with Digital Equipment

Corporation and working lots of hours. Still, I couldn't resist the appeal of channeling some of the energy I had into trying to make a go of an entrepreneurial venture. Two things happened to push me over the edge into the lifestyle I now have. In early 1983 my company announced an employee purchase program that would facilitate employee purchase of its new PC equipment at a 50 percent discount with attractive financing options also available. In addition, the district for which I worked was relocating to a new facility. Because this was during the booming 1980s, the relocation was accompanied by a plan to replace all of the office furnishings. I volunteered to assist some of my colleagues in organizing a giant corporate "tag sale" to dispose of all the "old" furniture (most of which was in excellent condition). For our efforts we received "pick of the litter" and could purchase at very favorable rates choice-quality furniture. (I discuss in chapter 3 the details of how I put together my physical office.)

Once I established a corner in my basement with my "new" furniture and DECmate computer system (with then state-of-the-art letter-quality printer), I was ready to launch a business venture by October 1983. Admittedly, this is not the conventional way of going into business. But I've learned from talking with many other service providers in this industry that certain pivotal circumstances often provide an underlying incentive to starting a company.

A colleague from work (who became my husband a few years later) volunteered to post notices about my "typing service" around the campus of the university where he was attending classes during the evening. This resulted in my first client in November 1983 (for a lengthy term paper). This project, billed at my hourly rate of $10, grossed me $74 . . . and was my only revenue for the fiscal year ending 1983 (actually, just a six-week period of time). I started slowly, while continuing to work full-time hours by day. I made the wise decision in the spring of 1984 to install a business telephone line and also arranged for two Yellow Pages ads under Typing Service and Resumes. Interestingly, these continue to be my two strongest categories for pulling first-time clients today.

I handled a few more projects throughout the spring and summer of 1984, and finally the updated annual telephone directory carrying my ads was published in September 1984. Then the telephone began to ring . . . and it's fair to say it really hasn't stopped ringing since (except for the intervals around my two relocations that followed—from Connecticut to Boston in 1986, and back to Connecticut in 1988).

Throughout these early years I continued to maintain my full-time position at Digital (with a few promotions along the way). Relying on my answering machine to take calls during the business day, I would utilize my lunch hour to go to a pay phone and dial in with my remote playback device to obtain messages left in the morning—and quickly return those calls. I also met with clients at a McDonald's located near my office, conducting business in a booth. The minute I'd get home from work, I would check the answering machine again and return the afternoon calls. Thus, callers would have a gap of at most five or six hours between leaving a message and receiving a return call.

For the majority it was transparent that I was working full time away from my home office during the day. Was this easy? Absolutely not. But it allowed me to start and build the business slowly, while still having the security and benefits of a full-time position. It was during this time that I was also able to avail myself of lots of relevant training programs in the areas of human resources, interviewing, and people development—all skills needed for my position by day (by then I'd been promoted into management), while at the same time rounding out my skill set for the work I ultimately wanted to do: providing resume consultation and interview training services as a component of my overall business.

It wasn't until my twins were born in 1987 that I determined my own personal objectives (staying home with my children) and plans for my business (taking it to full-time status) could be enacted in one fell swoop: I opted not to return to my corporate position after my maternity leave ended.

Because my decision to go full time with my business coincided with a move back to my native Connecticut, I had my third (and hopefully final) opportunity to "restart" the business (as well as a third baby!). I enacted most of the advice I provide in this book to kick things off quickly. A *major* handicap: we moved in September 1988, missing publication of my advertising in the Yellow Pages by one full year. The first book I could get into was not distributed until September 1989. So, as you read through this text, keep in mind that while I began under what I consider to be "worst-case scenario" for starting a secretarial service business (poor timing with publication of the Yellow Pages), there were still many inventive programs I implemented to jump-start the business successfully.

And it did happen quickly. The first few years back in Connecticut with newborn twins and a newly reborn business passed in nearly a blur. Thank goodness I shot a roll of film about every week for several years . . . and kept a good journal of my babies' progress! One year after the Yellow Pages advertising first appeared in September 1989, my revenues exceeded what I'd been earning in "the real world." I'd achieved my preliminary goal: staying home with my babies while making decent money. The business has only continued to grow, experiencing outstanding growth each year since hitting that important first-year threshold. About the only things I miss from the corporate world are the daily in-person contacts one has with numerous colleagues and the opportunities for travel. A relatively small trade-off, in my opinion. I relish my independence, love the widely diversified and interesting projects I handle, thoroughly enjoy my wonderful clients, and am thrilled with the financial rewards.

On the personal side—I'm a lot more available to my family than I would be under any other working scenario. I have complete flexibility with regard to taking the time my family or I need for everything from childbirth, vacation, and an hour out in the garden to caring for the three kids when they all had chicken pox, scheduling the time I needed to write this book, and fitting in daily swimming lessons for two-week intervals throughout the summer. With advance planning, tight scheduling, and excellent client communications, anything is possible with this business. No employer I know would be nearly as accommodating, yet I sustain 100 percent productivity and solid profitability. Adding in the sheer pleasure that comes from providing top-notch services that please clients and knowing you're doing excellent work that you truly love—what, I ask you, could be better?

I hope I've inspired you . . . and I promise to provide as much support, encouragement, and practical ideas and recommendations as I possibly can in the chapters that follow to encourage *you* to begin!

All this will not be finished in the first one hundred days.

Nor will it be finished in the first one thousand days. . . .

But let us begin.

> — JOHN FITZGERALD KENNEDY, *Inaugural Address*
> (January 20, 1961)

1

Preliminaries and Assumptions

Welcome

Congratulations on your decision to investigate starting a home-based secretarial service. The first steps are usually the most difficult. This book is designed to provide specific information to help ease your transition into successful business ownership in the months—and years—ahead.

There are probably an infinite number of reasons for wanting to start a home-based business providing secretarial and office support services; perhaps some of these points describe you:

- You possess specialized secretarial skills and a strong administrative background.

- You already own some or all of the necessary equipment.

- You would like to leave the "corporate rat race" and capitalize on your experience.

- You have young children—or plan to have them—and want to take advantage of the flexibility a home-based business affords.
- You have decided that working for someone else is not as appealing as working for yourself.
- You have informally been typing "this or that" for any number of people over the years and decided that it now makes sense to structure what you've been doing all along by calling it a business, charging for your services, and growing it into a truly viable business.
- You are an empty-nester—maybe your children are now grown, or perhaps you opted not to have children—and have decided that growing a business from your home appeals to you.
- You want to capitalize on the potential to earn more money and achieve greater job satisfaction than you've been able to in the past.
- You have an unused room and a need to earn some extra money and have decided a home-based business might be the solution—plus offer tax advantages you've often considered investigating.
- You are newly retired—or about to retire—but wish neither to give up a full-time income nor to be tied down to a full-time position working for someone else.
- You recognize that you've always had "entrepreneurial blood" running through your veins and that there's no time like the present to start to enact the dream you've always had to own your own business.

These are all good reasons to consider starting a home-based secretarial service. With in-depth investigation and planning, the appropriate level of skills, seed money for start-up costs and equipment, and possibly more energy, motivation, hard work, and enthusiasm than you've ever channeled toward a "job" before, you will find it possible to realize the professional and financial success as well as experience the high degree of satisfaction that accompanies the achievement of a goal of this magnitude.

This book is designed to provide you with proven techniques

and key information culled from my experience as well as the experiences of many other successful home-based secretarial service owners. Specific details are included that will guide you through every step of starting and running a successful business.

Assessing Personal/Career Short- and Long-term Goals

Let's get down to specifics . . . and reflect back on the earlier possibilities mentioned for wishing to start a home-based secretarial service. Keep in mind as you work your way through the questions that these are simply discussion points to consider, both personally and perhaps with family members. Remember that anyone sharing the same home from which you plan to operate a home-based business will be affected by your decisions. There are no right or wrong answers to these questions. They are essentially guidelines to understanding the reasons underlying your desire to own a business and may highlight certain areas that could present special challenges to you in the future as your business grows. Jot down on paper your thoughts in response to each of the following points—and save this information for later reference.

1. Consider the importance to you of being your own boss and reporting to no one other than yourself. Is this extremely important to you—or not that important?

2. Consider the ability to have unlimited income potential (you may see this claim appearing in magazine advertisements, but in this business it really is possible, with certain constraints— number of hours you are willing to work; external factors, such as whether you have young children in your home; client base; and so on). Is this extremely important to you—or not that important?

3. Consider the flexibility of your work schedule, from the standpoint of hours, days, and weeks that you choose to work. Also

consider being the individual who determines those things and has the ability to change them almost at a moment's notice. In other words, you set and alter the schedule to suit your needs. For everyone from women with young children at home to retirees wishing to remain "footloose and fancy-free" as they travel periodically throughout the year, a home-based business can ideally provide the necessary flexibility. Is this extremely important to you—or not that important?

4. For many business owners there is a great deal of pride and self-esteem that accompanies being able to say, "I own my own company." Is this extremely important to you—or not that important?

These are the primary areas that most home-based business owners cite when asked why they started their own companies. They are also an individual reflection of your own personal goals and values in life. These create a good framework for discussions with other family members as you explore your own reasons for establishing a business.

Legal Technicalities and Zoning Issues to Consider

Before plunging into the secondary level of concerns related to starting a successful business, you must address several critical issues early on in the process. First, you must ascertain if your proposal to operate a home-based secretarial service is sanctioned within your own city or town's planning and zoning regulations. Your city or town clerk's office can serve as the best source of information in order to begin the application process. As home-based businesses have proliferated through the 1980s and 1990s, so too have the regulations and application processes developed that are designed to contain and control them within many municipalities nationwide.

Typically, most towns will require that you complete a simple, one-page application that details the type of home-based business you wish to operate. Two or three lines are all that would be required, such as "Home-based secretarial and office support services. Will meet with clients on an individual basis, occasionally in their offices and occasionally in my home office. Will provide professional word processing/typewriting/desktop publishing services." There are generally several key areas with which most local agencies are primarily concerned:

1. That you do not plan to operate a business in which there will be associated disturbing noises or smells, use or produce any type of hazardous chemicals or materials, or create any other type of potentially hazardous condition.

2. That you do not plan to operate a business that could in any way disrupt the neighborhood in which you live, create a nuisance situation, or alter the character of the community.

3. That you do not plan to operate a business in which significant traffic and associated problems would be a component.

4. That you do not plan to operate a business that will have many or, in some communities, any employees.

5. That you do not plan to install any form of signage beyond what is permitted. In some communities no outside visible signage is allowed, particularly if you reside in a town's historic district or in a condominium association or apartment complex. In other areas specific size limitations are provided for the posting of one business sign.

6. That you do not plan to operate a business that occupies more than a certain percentage of space available in your total living area (generally, a home-based business must occupy 25 percent or less of the total living space). A simple hand-sketched map, depicting your proposed office space as it relates to the overall size of your dwelling (using square-footage measurements), is generally required.

7. That if you own your home, you can demonstrate appropriate parking, if requested. Using an A2 survey map, as-built plan, or plot plan that shows your house, the portion of your house proposed for your business and the proposed parking for your clientele should be depicted. The parking plan for a business of this type is quite basic: typically indicating that no more than one client will be visiting your office at a time, together with a statement that "ample parking is available in the driveway, along a street, or in a parking area."

8. That signatures of approval have been collected from adjacent neighbors attesting to their support of (or lack of objection to) your operating a home-based business.

9. That you have included the small fee accompanying the application that is generally required (usually between $20 and $50). This should be your first business expense; you don't want to expend money on expensive business cards, stationery, and a telephone line if you haven't ensured that operating a home business in your community is permitted by the zoning regulations. Until such time that you have selected your permanent business name and opened a checking account, you should use your own personal checks, carefully annotated to reflect the business costs incurred (and retaining the checks once canceled). These later become deductible expenses for your income tax return.

If you have a business plan or outline, this can become part of the zoning application package, but it is generally not required. (Chapter 3 discusses development of a business plan in detail.)

When you initially obtain the blank application form, you will be advised of the procedure for submitting the application package. You will probably be asked to attend a meeting of the planning and zoning commission for your town. You should ask to have sent to you a copy of the agenda for the meeting at which your application will be discussed; you should also plan to attend that meeting. While practices vary from city to city, you may be asked to briefly explain the nature of the application to the commission chartered to review home-based business applications. You would simply respond by reading from the description you have provided on the application.

Once you have secured approval from your town to operate your business, you should check with the secretary of state's office regarding registration of your business name (see chapter 3 regarding selection of your business name). Again, your city or town hall can provide valuable assistance in completing what is known as a "trade name certificate." The information you must provide includes the type of business (secretarial/word processing service), name you have selected for the business, address of the business, and your name; the city or town clerk will notarize the certificate. There is typically a small filing fee (approximately $20).

At this time you should also investigate obtaining a sales and use tax permit registration number (if your state requires that sales tax be collected on the type of services you plan to provide; this varies). Your town or city hall can provide information, as can your accountant, if you choose to have one. I have been in business since 1983 and not utilized the services of an accountant; however, I became acquainted very early on with my town clerk and have found her to be an excellent source of information regarding the types of documents I was required to complete as a start-up business owner. Provided that you determine a sole proprietorship is the optimum form of business organization (discussed in chapter 3), your social security number serves as your tax identification number.

Your city or town will also require you to complete a "Personal Property Declaration" form. This document is required so that local taxes can be assessed on your business equipment. Information that will be requested on the form includes your name and address, the business name and type of business, the type of ownership of the business (sole proprietorship, partnership, or corporation; as mentioned above, this is discussed in chapter 3), the date you physically occupied your dwelling, the overall square footage of the dwelling, and the purchase value of your business equipment and furnishings.

A second form accompanying the declaration, typically called

Sample Zoning Permit Application

Town of _____

Date _____   Fee _____

OWNER: _____   **APPLICANT:** _____
(your name)   (your name)

Address _____   Address _____

_____   _____

Phone _____   Phone _____

Affected Address___ (same as above) ___   Block # _____ Lot # _____
                                                      (above information available through your city or
                                                      town's land records)

APPLICATION FOR (check the block for "Home Occupation")

Approvals from (various city/town agencies . . . leave blank for their initials upon approval)

Current Use ___ (residence) _____

Proposed Use It is my intention to operate a secretarial service from my residence located at (specific address). The proposed office is located on the first floor, adjacent to the living room (or wherever you've decided to place it). There is a separate entrance serving the proposed office (or the entrance is through the existing front door of the dwelling). No physical alterations to the outside of the dwelling are planned; there will not be any external evidence of the business that would change the residential character of the dwelling.

The office occupies 10% of the total dwelling living area (or whatever the percentage, usually cannot exceed 25%), approximately 400 square feet (again, the specific number should be calculated). No employees are planned at this time. A sign in accordance with the regulations is planned for the future. Ample off-street parking is available for clients; it is anticipated that there might be several clients stopping by the office in a given day to deliver work or pick up completed materials. This business will not have a deleterious effect on the neighborhood and its property values. This home business will not cause an increase in traffic-producing safety hazards. A site plan of the neighborhood (can be your own drawing) is attached; it also details the site plan of the house and parking area (again, can be drawn by hand).

The following neighbors own property adjacent to the proposed home business (list names and addresses) and (if required) have signed the attached sheet demonstrating their support/approval of this proposed home occupation.

(A clause is generally included requesting you to attest to the accuracy of all information provided.)

Your signature/date _____

Zoning Enforcement Officer/date _____

"Confidential Information Report—Manufacturers, Merchants, and Traders," will require you to repeat most of the above information and indicate for each piece of business furniture and electronic/computer equipment the year acquired and the purchase price. A depreciation schedule is provided, and you will be asked to calculate the depreciated value. For example, if you purchased a $2,000 computer in 1992, the depreciated value (as per the percentage listed on the form) might be 80 percent in 1995; therefore, the number you would list under depreciated value would be $1,600. This number is then used as the basis for your personal property tax (if your locale assesses one; most communities do).

Once again, your best resource in determining the types of information required by your town or city would be your accountant or your city or town clerk.

2

Quotient for Home-based Business Success

At this point we've reviewed the basic information essential to knowing that it is legal and viable to operate a home-based secretarial service in your community. Now you can continue the evaluation process regarding your "quotient for home-based business success."

Again, this is not a scientific process; rather, it is an exploratory path for understanding your unique strengths (and weaknesses) and then utilizing this knowledge to best establish and position your business for success. Review your earlier notes about why you want to be in business for yourself. Then consider the following discussion areas.

Conducting a Skills Assessment

Evaluating what skills you possess is important, from knowing your keyboarding speed to understanding your style in dealing with problem situations. Being a successful business owner involves managing many tasks simultaneously, some of which you may never before have had the opportunity to handle. Most people considering an entrepreneurial career providing secretarial services have office experience, usually as a secretary or an administrative assistant. Many take for granted their skill at the keyboard but often overlook their lack of experience in the critical business areas of planning, marketing, sales, and customer service. Your skill in handling deadlines, dealing effectively with irate clients, managing customer relations, and solving problems is nearly as important as the professional techniques you will use in properly typing and formatting your clients' work.

Owning and operating your own business means that you will be wearing many and probably all of the following hats, at least in the first few years.

- You'll be required to be the president and CEO when it comes to decision making, long-term planning, and strategizing for your company's growth and future.

- You'll be the controller and manager of the Accounts Receivables Department when it comes to decisions regarding granting credit, pursuing slow-paying accounts, and terminating service for nonpayment.

- You'll be the director of public relations, marketing, and advertising when decisions need to be made concerning those publications in which to advertise, what organizations in the community to support, which direct mail pieces to implement, and how much money to spend on Yellow Pages advertising.

- You'll be the sales manager—doing all cold calling, promoting, cultivating of potential leads (every client is first a lead or a prospect), and selling of your business services. (P.S. This *never* ends, even when you've been in business five, ten, or more years. There will always be the need to cultivate new business.)

- You'll be the Customer Service Department manager, handling all client issues—work orders, scheduling matters, problems, corrections—*and* receiving those "Project looks great!" kudos from satisfied clients.

- You'll be the computer/software technician, learning and becoming proficient in the frequently complex systems and software you'll need to professionally produce your clients' materials.

- You'll be the receptionist, greeting each visitor to your office and every caller by phone.

- You'll be the supply clerk, maintaining a reasonable but not overly costly supply of inventory.

- You'll be the billing clerk, handling all invoicing promptly to ensure a healthy cash flow for your business.

- You'll be the repair technician, replacing used toners, cartridges, and printer ribbons; adjusting copy quality; and the like.

- You'll be the cleaning person, emptying the trash each night, dusting the office surfaces each day, placing a fresh flower on the desk in the morning, and running the vacuum over the floors to maintain a professional office appearance in your home office.

- If you're a parent with young children or a caregiver for an elderly parent residing in your home, you'll be managing the challenges of integrating your family responsibilities with growing your business.

- *And* you'll be what you probably describe yourself as—a crackerjack typist/word processor who wants to operate a successful home-based business!

In which of the above areas do you have practical experience? Where are your talents at the expert level? Consider all of the positions you've held in your career. Don't overlook any expertise you might have acquired in a volunteer capacity that would be relevant, such as the cold calling involved in fund-raising for a nonprofit organization.

In what areas might you require some additional assistance or training? For many entrepreneurs the sales aspect of their business is the most difficult. This book later delves into marketing, promotion, and sales in great detail and will provide you with lots of easy-to-implement, creative, and time-tested techniques to help you with effectively marketing your own business. There are also many

excellent publications available through the Small Business Administration (SBA) and on the shelves of your local library or bookstore
to give you added inspiration; see also this book's suggestions for
periodicals to consult/subscribe to (listed in the Appendix).

Reviewing Minimum Requirements and Analyzing Your Style

If you research start-up businesses (in any field, not just the secretarial services business), you'll quickly find that a significant
percentage fail within the first year . . . and probably only 10 percent of those started will still be in business five years later. Dismal
statistics! You can greatly optimize your chances for success in a
number of ways, not the least of which is comparing your skill set
against the minimum requirements outlined below. This listing of
skills is aggressive—and if your skills fall short, even in a number
of areas, don't become discouraged. This does not necessarily
mean that you're doomed for failure before starting. What follows
is, however, a realistic appraisal of some of the "given" attributes
a successful secretarial service owner should possess—or work to
improve—in starting a business.

Keyboard Skills

The suggested *minimum* words per minute that you should be able
to accurately type is 70. While it's possible to operate a service typing at a lower speed, recognize that your earnings will be
significantly less than for an individual who can type 90, 100, or
110 words per minute.

For example, the industry standard for producing eight pages
of double-spaced text is one hour. This is based on a typist with a
keyboard speed of 70 words per minute (assuming two to three
errors per page, frequently corrected in automated spellchecking
features typical with most computer word processing software).

If you have determined that your hourly rate, for the purposes
of this illustration, is $20 (information on determining appropriate

pricing appears in chapter 5), your charge to the client for this project, eight double-spaced pages, would be $20. Now, if you can type 90 words per minute, you would probably complete the project in forty-five minutes. Using industry standards, the fair charge for this project is one hour. Therefore, you would effectively "earn" $26 per hour. *But*, if you can only type 50 words per minute, the project is likely to take you one and one half hours. Because one hour is the standard for this work, your charge to the client should be $20, based on that being your hourly rate. Therefore, you would actually be earning only $13 an hour for your efforts.

Many other factors are taken into account when considering industry standards. Industry production standards have been developed by the National Association of Secretarial Services (NASS; information in the Appendix) for use by members of this professional association for the secretarial services industry. The standards provide information for fairly assessing the time necessary to perform specific work within certain parameters.

Industry standards in many industries have been developed for the benefit of both the customer or client and the service provider. By using standards, superior typists avoid penalizing themselves. In looking at the example provided, if the 90-words-per-minute typist charged just for the actual time of forty-five minutes expended on that project, instead of using the industry standard of one hour, the charge to the client would be $15 (three-quarters of an hour at the $20-per-hour rate). Utilizing standards is fair to the client and to the service provider.

Skill with the English Language

While some clients may insist that you type material exactly as they have presented it, the majority will welcome your "automatic" correction of any errors—spelling, punctuation, grammar, vocabulary, syntax. Most secretarial services do not charge extra for correcting these types of errors in client work. Obviously, if significant editing is necessary (and this should always be authorized by the client first), an additional fee is appropriate. But simply spelling words properly and using correct punctuation are typically expected by a client engaging the services of a professional secretarial service.

Your strong command of the English language is an asset to your clients. If you have particular expertise in this area and perhaps are a writer as well, your skills can naturally lend themselves to an additional profit center for your business—editorial services.

A Word about Profit Centers

Profit centers are specific areas of business that can be segregated for the purpose of reporting and collecting data on your expenses and your revenues. For example, if you have a copy machine in your office and provide copies to clients, the charges for copies should be noted separately on invoices (more on this later) and tracked as an individual profit center. You should also be tracking your costs for the copier separately (lease expense or purchase cost, paper and toner expenses, and service calls or maintenance contract expense). At year's end you will know, for the "Copy Profit Center," exactly what your expenses were to provide this service as well as your income from this service. This same formula holds true for every aspect of your business—from tracking stationery costs and fax services to producing a breakout of your hourly rates for different services (see Recordkeeping in chapter 5).

Proofreading Skills

Automated spellchecking features in word processing programs have removed some of the need for proofreading for misspelling of words in documents. Most spellcheckers, however, are not sophisticated enough to notice a dropped ending on a word (you typed *possess* when the word should be *possesses*). Nor can a spellchecker alert you to dropped text (when typing a lengthy document containing repetitive terminology, you glanced away from the original page, and when you looked back, your eyes picked up the word you just typed—*neuropsychological*—but at a different place on the page). These examples point out the continued need for excellent proofreading ability.

Of course, there will be occasions when you are asked to prepare a draft document and use computer spellchecking only—the client is planning to edit anyway and will catch typographical errors during that review process. You should factor in time proof-reading all other work, however, with particular emphasis placed on resumes and cover letter materials. The hallmark of a great secretarial service is the ability to produce work professionally, promptly, and *accurately*. While everyone is human and will make an occasional error that will slip through even the best spellchecking system and careful proofreading, the successful business owner wants to keep these to a minimum.

Visual Layout Ability

Although this skill is somewhat intangible and difficult to define, most successful secretarial service owners recognize the need for producing work that is not only accurate and to a client's specifications but visually appealing as well. While a true graphic arts background isn't essential (although a plus if you have it and an ideal add-on profit center!), formatting text and layout as well as determining font size and any special design elements require an eye for detail and visual appeal. This includes such formatting features as italicizing, using bold, using a lighter font, using a contrasting font, underscoring, and indenting. Two documents perfectly typed can look entirely different depending on the typist's ability to employ good visual layout. Over time your skill in this area will be rewarded by a reputation for producing work that not only is accurate but looks professional too. This emphasis is reflected in my business slogan: *"Our Business Is Making You Look Good!"* Many of my clients over the years have either their own computers or their own secretaries . . . yet still utilize my services. Why? They tell me it's because "You work 'magic' and make me look good."

Math Aptitude

This is a fundamental requirement—from the standpoint of both managing your business's financial health and working with clients. A small calculator is essential. You may periodically be required to calculate or verify statistical information in client materials. You will probably need to calculate sales tax on most if not all of your services and products sold (paper supplies, postage, etc.). You need to feel comfortable with handling at least the preliminary accounting for your business so that you can quickly spot trends, respond to projected cash-flow crunches, and so forth.

Interpersonal and Communications Skills

Probably even more important than your computer/keyboarding skill and technical know-how is your ability to deal effectively with people. Providing secretarial services will expose you to many types of people. From professionals and white-collar senior management types to college and graduate students to blue-collar laborers and gray-collar techni-professionals, you will be in contact with all of these people throughout nearly every business day. Your ability to "change hats" and relate with impact *and* empathy will largely govern your overall business success.

Why is this so important? The services you provide are a commodity—secretarial services are probably available from a number of sources in your area. Why do people choose to do business with the firms they do? *People.* You are what will make your business a true success. Your ability to make all clients comfortable, secure, and confident in your ability to handle their work—and to follow through on your promises—is what will make for repeat business and build that all-important client base. Likewise, satisfied clients will do the single thing that's most important for your business growth (besides pay for your services)—*they'll tell others.* No other advertising is as important as the referrals your happy clients will provide (more on this later).

The more genuinely interested you are in your clients' businesses, the more valuable they will perceive you. Your aspiration should be to be a team player with each of your clients. For example, with every resume client you handle—even those merely having their resume typeset exactly as they've written it—you want to convey your sense of involvement and caring. When a resume client contacts you several weeks after the initial resume/cover letter project to ask for your assistance in preparing additional cover letters, you should express interest in the previous correspondence the person sent seeking interviews. "How did that opportunity at the university turn out for you?" Your ability to utilize quick memory recall can be a real plus here! I have a very poor memory—but a good filing system that enables me to quickly pull out a paper file for each resume client with copies of the correspondence and resume attached. This prompts me in asking appropriate questions.

Likewise, with your business/corporate clientele, staying abreast of their industry or field is equally important. "What did the results of the survey reveal?" might follow a survey project for a business client in your next telephone contact. "How was your lecture received?" "How did that sales call at XYZ Company go?" Whatever could logically follow a project you handled recently is the perfect question to ask in a follow-up call (whether initiated by you or the client). We're all flattered when people remember what we do and those activities in which we're involved. Clients will be impressed by your interest in their business.

Professional Demeanor and Polish

Establishing a professional presence from a home office setting can be challenging for some. I am firmly of the belief that if you are *always* professional in your client dealings, produce a top-quality product, and cultivate solid working relationships with your clients, you will naturally convey a highly professional demeanor. Whether you choose to dress in a corporate suit or a jogging suit is your decision . . . and you have the flexibility, from a home office, to quickly change to appropriately meet the requirement. For example, when meeting with a first-time corporate client in my home office, I always assume a more traditional "corporate" look. I've long since disposed of my constricting matched-jacket-and-skirt business suits, but I do have a nice wardrobe of unconstructed jackets, coordinating skirts, and the like. The same is true when meeting with a resume client who is a professional (information exchanged in the preliminary call to my office typically reveals something of the person's background; when I know that I'm meeting with a health care professional to update her CV [curriculum vitae, as resumes are typically called in the health care, education, and psychological professions], I "dress the part."). I will also dress down ("professionally and neatly casual") when I'm meeting with a student to discuss typing a thesis or when a factory laborer is meeting with me early in the morning following his third-shift job.

Believe me, I don't spend a lot of conscious time on this aspect of business—it has evolved naturally, and occasionally, I do err. Although all appointments are scheduled and I don't offer drop-in times, clients will periodically swing by to drop off a project if they are in the area. They may not expect to see me and simply plan to use a drop-off envelope I provide at the door. But they may catch me on a "writing" day when I have only a few client appointments scheduled with professional clients that work from home offices (and dress casually, as do I, for our meetings). I may be barefoot and dressed in shorts and a T-shirt, but I accord them the same respect, friendliness, and professionalism as I do when "dressed for business." Our relationship does not in any way suffer; in fact, many of the professionals with whom I work frequently sigh and tell me how much they admire the ability I have to work comfortably from my home office.

Professionalism is an attitude—how you convey it is a skill of combining words, direct eye contact, open body language, and a genuine appreciation for and respect of your clientele. Enough on this!

Customer Satisfaction

Your commitment to delivering customer satisfaction cannot be overemphasized. When you were working for someone else, chances are good that "the buck" did not stop with you; there was always someone higher in the organizational chain to whom you could refer problems during a customer dispute. When you are the business owner, all issues, positive and negative, typically start *and* stop with you. Your ability to diffuse a hot situation in which a client is agitated is critical. Your ability to remain objective and not be overly sensitive *or* defensive is just as key. The bottom line in any strong business is pleasing the customer . . . the adage we've all learned: "The customer is always right." No one wants unhappy clients—and we'll do all that is within our power to make a client satisfied.

If you are facing a situation in which a client has a complaint, be open and receptive to hearing and really listening to what the client is saying. Whether or not you believe there actually is a problem is irrelevant. If a client says there is a problem, then there is a problem. Your objective should be to discover as quickly and calmly as possible how the situation can be remedied. For an obvious problem, such as a typographical error appearing on a resume, a simple correction is all that is in order (accompanied by profuse apologies; by a reminder—if applicable—that the client did have an opportunity to review and approve the proof copy prior to printing and therefore must assume the cost of the correction, if a large number of originals are involved; and by a quick repair).

In some cases it may make the most sense for you to absorb the cost of correcting a typographical error, even if you do include on your work order a statement that "final proofreading is the responsibility of the client" (more information on this in chapter 5 under Organization—Client Work Order). Client goodwill and word of mouth are worth protecting at nearly any price. Because you are the boss, you can adjust your own rules at any time. It's well worth your quarter-hour of time to make a free correction and provide twenty newly printed laser originals of the corrected resume at no charge—graciously, courteously, smiling all the time—to a client who is highly and perhaps irrationally irate. After all, what ill will is a client likely to spread when you've bent over backward to appease and satisfy the person?

Business analysts have calculated that, in terms of money and time, it costs nearly four times as much to cultivate a new client as it does to retain an existing client. If you already have a client through the door, it's much more effective to work with that client to resolve a dispute than it is to begin the sales process all over again with someone new. Of course, as in any other aspect of life, there may be the occasion when you simply don't value a particular client's work enough to make it worth the aggravation . . . and would prefer to not handle the work. In this case there may not be a personality fit between you and the client, the client may be one of those fortunately rare individuals that simply can't be pleased, and you determine it is not of mutual benefit to cultivate a relationship any longer. In that case my recommendation is to indicate professionally that continuing a business relationship appears not to be in the best interest of either party and to provide a referral to another service. No law requires you to work with any client. If you've entered into a relationship, plans do need to be made for ceasing that particular business arrangement, including a reasonable period of time for notice; provision of work completed to date and of disk copies, if appropriate; return of client stationery; final payment of account; and so forth. In my years of being in business since 1983, I've never had this scenario play out. But I do have colleagues in this business who have done just this to absolve themselves of such a difficulty.

Marketing and Sales Skills

Polished marketing skills, the ability to promote yourself and your business, and the capability of selling are all important attributes to developing and maintaining a successful business. While probably only a few lucky entrepreneurs naturally possess these skills and attributes, the rest of us can quickly learn and develop our techniques in this area. Just by implementing many of the ideas appearing in chapter 4, you will become more comfortable with the function of marketing for your secretarial services business. And there's truth in the phrase "Nothing succeeds like success." As you capture new business, successfully turning callers into clients, you'll develop "recyclable" phrases and terminology that you can use again and again in speaking on the phone. Far from sounding "programmed," you'll develop a professional polish that is conveyed to the listener.

Many periodicals devote monthly columns to the topic of marketing (some of the best for the secretarial services industry are listed in the Appendix); bookstore and library shelves overflow with books proclaiming the virtues of their own techniques for enhancing your ability to promote and sell your business. The Appendix includes the titles of just a sampling of some of the best of these books. Pore through your own favorite bookstore and public library shelves to unearth others. Keep in mind too that professional periodicals to which you subscribe can become tax deductions for your business. So too can the professional seminars and programs you are encouraged to attend in your locale—they have double impact, educating you through exposure to different marketing ideas and providing you with valuable opportunities for networking with other professionals and possible clients in your community.

Check with the Business Development Office in your city (or nearest large city) for additional information. The SBA office in your area can also provide information about upcoming seminars. Local colleges and universities frequently offer programs in conjunction with the SBA. Local telephone companies may also offer programs for developing your business that you would find beneficial. I try to attend at least two professional workshops or conventions per year, including one in our industry (NASS sponsors an outstanding convention each year, and local chapters also host regional annual conferences; see the Appendix).

Desire to Be Successful . . . and Drive to Work Hard

This may be an understatement, for to be truly successful, you must sincerely *want* success. Success must be defined in your *own* words. For most secretarial service owners, the ultimate plan is to work a full-time schedule (or perhaps slightly less) for *greater*-than-full-time pay in relation to a comparable position in a company. For example, if as a secretary a person earned $25,000 for working a typical 8:30 to 5:00, five-day-a-week job, as the owner of a business this person would want to have as a salary (*not* the revenues of the business, out of which must come taxes, expenses, and all other costs of doing business) at least $25,000, generally $35,000 or $40,000, and optimistically anywhere up to $50,000 or $75,000 or even $100,000! These numbers should, of course, be adjusted for your geographic area of the country and whether or not you live in or near a large metropolitan area. Essentially, the potential is limited only by you and your desire to build your business.

Many entrepreneurs have as a realistic goal working *fewer hours* than they did in what I like to call "the real world," while at the same time earning *more money*. This is a great goal and highly achievable, with hard work and planning, particularly at the outset.

It's a fair statement, and you'll hear it from every successful entrepreneur, that you will work harder building your business and for yourself than you ever have in the past. But you'll also derive infinitely greater job satisfaction and, hopefully, more income than you ever did working for someone else. There are probably no successful entrepreneurs in any field doing what they love who dread "going to work." For most of us it's a pleasure to be in our offices, working with clients, doing work we enjoy, and receiving good money for it. In fact, for many of us where a key difficulty can rear its head is in finding the all-important balance necessary to sustain a life *and* a business.

For many successful entrepreneurs the tendency to be a perfectionist is a natural characteristic. It's easy to get carried away with working too much when your business is thriving and reaching a point of where you must make critical decisions regarding its overall future as you manage its growth. We'll talk more about this later. For most budding entrepreneurs dealing with too *much* work is a problem they would love to manage in the first year!

Ambition and Inner Motivation

When you answer to only your clients and ultimately yourself, you must have within you the pride that is associated with owning your own business. No one will criticize you in your performance evaluation for taking too many sick days (clients may complain and, worse, go elsewhere, but there's no one to dock your pay if you decide not to show up for work one day; however, in this business if you aren't working, you aren't generating what are known as "billable hours"). This is not to say that it isn't appropriate to take well-deserved days off. They simply must be planned reasonably in advance if you have clients that utilize your service very regularly and on appointed days.

High energy level and good health should accompany your own motivation and drive to succeed. You'll need these characteristics as your business grows. The work of a secretarial service is generally not able to be grouped into perfect work segments. Some periods of the year will find you overwhelmed if you accept student work on top of regular client requirements, particularly during term paper or thesis season at a nearby university. You'll pull "all-nighters" characteristic of when you were back in college. Other times of the year may find you working at less than capacity. For some secretarial service owners, the weeks between Thanksgiving and Christmas are characteristically slow, as are the months of July and August. Once your business has hit its stride, you'll welcome these brief respite periods. They allow for the necessary time to rejuvenate your batteries and devote resources to strategically planning your business.

Years ago I used to panic if I looked at my daily to-do list (see Other Relevant Forms—Project Status/Deadline Sheet in chapter 5) and had less than five or six client projects and deadlines listed. I'd worry that I would run out of work. For at least five years, I really haven't had the pleasure of thinking I might run out of work for a day or two and actually have time to catch up on some of my filing for the business . . . or play with a new software program . . . or experiment with a different layout for my company's newsletter. Now the only time my to-do list ever has fewer than ten or fifteen projects on it is when I'm gearing up for a vacation. Then I really have to work double time to accomplish all projects before leaving (and work twice as hard when returning to get back on track). But I'm calling the shots—and I love it!

I always advise newcomers to this industry to relish the times when things are relatively quiet. That's not to say that if your phone isn't ringing at all, you shouldn't be taking proactive steps to build your business. But if you've got a fairly regular client base and an expectation from regular clients of ongoing work, an occasional quiet day or two can provide essential time for refocusing and exercising continual development of your business. In the first few months and years, you should plan to spend a specified amount of time each day on marketing your business. More details are provided in chapter 4 as to the types of activities that can be most beneficial to growing your business.

Outstanding Organizational Ability

Being a home-based secretarial service owner, like any business owner, but especially those who are home-based, requires extraordinary skill in juggling multiple priorities, tasks, and work responsibilities. For those also caring for young children or aging parents, your management skills will be tested even more. But the rewards derived from operating a successful business in your home are unmatched, and throughout this text I'll provide many suggestions and tips for getting the most out of your valuable time.

Advantages and Drawbacks to Operating a Home-based Business

There are infinitely more advantages than disadvantages to owning a home-based secretarial service, but it's worthwhile to review both sides of the picture. First, the positive aspects of such an enterprise.

Advantages

- Because you will most likely be meeting with clients on an appointment-only basis (as opposed to a storefront operation, where drop-ins are common and the hours are generally fixed), you maintain greater flexibility over your own work schedule. This works particularly well in helping to balance business with your personal life. Whether it's taking an afternoon off occasionally to attend a professional meeting, go to a doctor's appointment, participate at your children's school, poke around in your garden or an antiques store, or simply do nothing, you are in charge of arranging your own schedule.

- Nothing beats the commute to a home-based business! This translates into significant savings in terms of the rent or leasing costs of an external office, commuting costs, professional wardrobe (you can get away with far fewer professional outfits when you're not appearing in the same business office five days a week), power lunches, and possibly day care (more in chapter 6 on this aspect of operating a business when you have young children).

- You directly control your income. Unless you were in sales, you probably had a fixed salary, little opportunity to earn bonuses, and waited twelve to eighteen months for an increase. When you own the business, you set the prices, determine the timing and amount of increases in your rates, and have the ability to aggressively market, offer promotions, and work harder/more hours to generate greater cash flow. Overtime in "the real world" was probably mandated or available only at your employer's discretion. Here you make the decisions when you will work and how much you will work.

- In this business you can opt to handle only the types of work you actually *like* handling. For some, transcription is a bore, difficult, or hated . . . so, your secretarial service doesn't have to provide this service. Maybe you dislike typing statistical copy—don't solicit this type of work. Perhaps your greatest enjoyment is working with lengthy manuscripts—you should actively seek this kind of work. Because you are the manager, you dictate what services your business will provide. Most brand-new secretarial service owners find they'll take any and all work in the initial months—and perhaps years—"as long as it's legal." As your business develops, however, you may find that specializing in certain areas of the business appeals to you and that doing certain work does not. You make the call!

- While you do have clients to "answer to," owning your own business provides the greatest flexibility in emergency situations. For me emergencies have ranged from simply being available to pick up a sick child at preschool on a moment's notice and having three preschoolers home over a period of six weeks as they all battled chicken pox (not quite simultaneously) to having a chance to get away last-minute for a week in the sun. All that I needed to do was coordinate my calendar with my clients', work more at night, and maintain regular communications. My former employers from the corporate world might not have been as flexible over a six-week hiatus with the chicken pox! My clients had no objection to meeting me on my porch (for those who hadn't been exposed) or in the evenings.

- There are significant tax advantages to owning your own business, particularly when it is home-based. While this book is not intended to provide specific legal or financial advice and you are encouraged to seek professional counsel in these areas, throughout the text I will share some of the benefits I've found in these areas.

- In addition to scheduling client meetings and appointments to suit your schedule, you also have the flexibility of determining the best times of day (or night) that you'd like to work. When my twins were infants, I found I worked during assorted pockets of the day and night, whenever they were napping or sleeping. Sometimes that meant I'd be at the computer from 5:00 A.M. until the next feeding at 8:30 A.M.; in other instances I'd sit down to work after the 11:00 P.M. feeding and work until their next feeding at 3:00 A.M. before I decided to retire for the night. As the children got older, my work habits changed to reflect my true biological clock—a night owl's. Unless I'm scheduled to meet with a client at 7:00 or 7:30 A.M., I generally am not at my desk until 8:00 A.M. But I nearly always work evenings until midnight, later if a deadline mandates. Because I have three preschoolers still home in the afternoons, I'm not able to work on a dedicated basis between 1:00 P.M. and suppertime. Herein lies the great flexibility of owning your own business. Whatever your particular lifestyle requirements, this business can flow right around it. Many of my colleagues are empty-nesters and keep more traditional business hours, rarely if ever working evenings or weekends. That's a future aspiration for my business!

Drawbacks

- Managing your personal and business time will probably be the single greatest hurdle facing you as a home-based secretarial service owner. While the flexibility such a business provides is wonderful for you, your clients may begin to think it is designed for them. In fact, when I first started my business I still held a full-time traditional day job. I could *only* meet with my clients after hours and on the weekends. I sold this as an *advantage* to them—"I'm available to meet with you during *your* off-hours so that you're not losing valuable business time." In the many years, however, since I took my business to a full-time status and gave up my external employment, I found clients still wanting to utilize the perceived advantage of my availability after hours. I'm flexible and structure my time to meet their needs, while at the same time being cautious not to let it spill too much into my family's time. This can be a constant struggle for some. (See Cultivating Client Relationships in chapter 5.) Many secretarial service owners describe their own experiences, some hilarious, in which they were disturbed at home on holidays, late in the evening (after going to bed), or in the early morning before they had dressed for business. About the latter I have my own funny story, which you can chuckle over in chapter 6.

- Security for a home-based business is paramount in the minds of many. Because many secretarial services businesses are owned by women who work from their homes, at least during the daytime hours, alone, it's important to give consideration to this and plan accordingly. I believe it's a fair statement that even in a traditional office setting or executive suite arrangement, it's impossible to prepare for all possible problems.

But you can take steps, as a home-based business owner, to ensure the greatest peace of mind and security for you, your home, and its assets. By not permitting drop-in appointments, you should never be surprised by an unannounced visitor. When scheduling appointments over the telephone, you will need to develop an almost "sixth sense" in discerning true callers (99 percent) from the occasional prankster. I make it a practice never to reveal my street address in any advertising (including Yellow Pages) or promotional literature; I utilize a post office box. When responding to a telephone inquiry from an unknown prospective client who has asked, "Where are you located?" I indicate that I am off the main street in my town. I quickly add that once we've discussed the person's requirements and are at the point where we are scheduling an appointment, I'll be happy to provide specific directions. A prankster is not going to engage in five minutes of telephone discussion over a nonexistent project simply to learn your address (at least that's been my finding). Use your own common sense and good judgment. There have been occasions when I've felt uncomfortable over the telephone, even after discussing a project. In such cases I then attempt to schedule an appointment at a time that I know either my children or, preferably, my husband will be here. I will also sometimes fictitiously state, "Yes, 3:00 will be a convenient time. My associate will be speaking with another client at that time, but the office is large and we can accommodate that." Only twice in my years of doing business have I actually asked a neighbor (retired and, incidentally, my father) to physically be present in the office during questionable appointments. I've never had a problem.

Some secretarial service owners I know have established a calling system with colleagues in their communities. Someone I know even went so far as to make a telephone connection with a neighbor by calling that person's number and leaving the telephone on her desk so that if a problem arose, she could simply scream and the telephone could transmit her plea for assistance to the neighbor listening on the other end. This is somewhat drastic, but whatever makes you most comfortable is worth doing. Many home-based businesses have installed professional security systems that include a feature whereby you can punch in a quick code in an emergency to alert a monitoring station that you're in distress. This can impart a feeling of confidence and security. Some secretarial service owners I know keep a radio turned to a talk station on low volume in a room adjacent to their office, to provide the illusion of someone else being in the home during their appointments.

Physical location of your office comes into play here as well. Ideally, you do not want to situate your office (at least the portion of your office where you will be meeting clients) in the bedroom or living areas of your home. The perfect location would be somewhere separate from these areas—a room adjacent to your home, a renovated garage or closed-in porch, or perhaps even a basement room (that's where I started out). In my own case, after outgrowing my basement quarters I moved with all my equipment to what was then a spare child's room. With the exception of one client who became a family friend, I never brought a client down to this "office"; instead, I always had all the necessary supplies for an initial client meeting at my dining room table, and that's where I met clients for several years, until the point where I had a large office constructed adjacent to my home. A disadvantage to not having your computer equipment in the same setting as where you meet clients is during those times when a quick correction is necessary while a client waits. By this time, though, the client is in the office for at least the second time, or maybe the third, and money has already exchanged hands. In such situations I always found I could comfortably (and quickly) scoot down to my bedroom office, make a change, and return to the dining room. I always provided relevant reading material and information for my clients to peruse while I was gone—and was never away for more than five minutes. If lengthy changes were required, I scheduled a follow-up appointment.

• Turning off your professional work self is more difficult when your work space is physically located in your home. In the early years this may not present itself as a problem, but as business grows you may find that it's hard to stay away from your desk—especially if your office is located in eyeshot of other living areas—when you have deadlines encroaching. Similar to managing client interruptions on your personal/family life, structuring time off for yourself and your family can be a challenge. Some secretarial service owners find it's useful to dedicate at least one day per week, and possibly two (frequently on the weekends), when they simply will not go into their offices, respond to messages on their answering machines, or "think" work at all. This type of discipline is not always easy to impose on yourself but should evolve quite naturally with time.

Entrepreneurial Analysis: Do You Have What It Takes to Be Successful Working for Yourself?

Unlike tests in school, this analysis isn't graded. Rather, as you respond to each of the questions and then read the profile of a typically successful entrepreneur, assess how you "stack up." This forms a good framework for understanding your strengths . . . and your potential weaknesses.

• How good is your health, and how much sleep do you require?

Entrepreneurial success will depend almost entirely on your efforts—including your ability to work hard and sustain momentum once your business is running smoothly and has a fairly regular cash flow. Do you have "staying power?" Are you able to pull occasional all-nighters when necessary? Are you in generally good health, and do you eat properly and exercise? These factors can all play into your general ability to maintain a successful business.

• At what age did you first begin to test the "entrepreneurial waters?" Did you deliver newspapers, babysit, wash pets or cars, organize tag sales, clean houses for pay, or sell juice drinks before you were old enough to hold a "real" part-time job?

Most successful entrepreneurs can recall evidence in their childhood of their ability to promote as well as their salesmanship. The thirst for being in business for oneself and making money begins early.

- Do you have a close relative who is or was a successful entrepreneur?

  Statistics have typically shown that "entrepreneurial blood" runs in families—or perhaps you are starting the trend in your family. In my own case my grandparents were successful restaurateurs, building a popular restaurant/banquet hall/resort in a remote area of Connecticut during the Great Depression, then growing it to success, operating it for fifty years. Even before that successful enterprise, my grandfather proved his entrepreneurial worth—and honed his sales skills—selling Watkins products for many years around the state of Connecticut. My dad also worked for himself successfully for nearly thirty years with a home-based office. Being an entrepreneur seemed the natural thing for me to do: I recall seeing my name inscribed after my dad's on the hallway leading downstairs to his basement office: "Manton H. LaFountain and Janice, Inc." I was probably four or five when I first understood what this meant.

- How competitive were you in organized school or college sports? Do you continue competitive involvement to this date?

  Once again, the "true blood" of an entrepreneur tends to become established early on. This relates to organized activities as well as business pursuits.

- What kind of a student were you?

  While excelling in English positions you for success in providing secretarial and editorial services, developing a new business and managing its myriad aspects—including accounting, reporting, and planning—rely heavily on your expertise in general business administration. Any training you may have had in business, accounting, management, and organization will be very useful.

- Are you an early riser or a night owl? Do you possess the ability to work for long stretches of time, seemingly without a break?

  Entrepreneurs tend to get so caught up in their business that they never watch clocks, except to be alert to appointments, and they frequently work both ends of the clock (called "burning the candle at both ends").

- How good is your memory? Or, phrased another way, do you have good work habits established with regard to making lists, maintaining a to-do list, and keeping a calendar?

  A successful secretarial service owner must manage many priorities, project deadlines, and appointments. Already being familiar with tracking time and making lists can be a real asset. Memory also plays a big role in learning more about your clients and their businesses. Many secretarial service owners track birthdates and other important dates in their clients' lives and send out greeting cards on a regular basis. Being able to ask a follow-up question or simply remembering at a Monday client appointment that the past weekend was the person's university's alumni weekend can put you in good stead with your client base. Become an avid user of the small, postage-stamp-size Post-It notes; use them everywhere as reminders!

- How much of a risk-taker are you?

  Starting any business is, of course, a risk. But beginning a secretarial service when you have assessed your skills and strengths can be an excellent venture and opportunity for you. As your business grows, will you continue to be willing to take risks? These can include the decisions to add new services and equipment as well as buying and learning new software. Being a successful entrepreneur almost goes hand in hand with being a calculated risk-taker.

- How well do you handle your personal finances? Are you organized? Do you reconcile your checkbook the minute the statement arrives? Do you pay your bills on time and avoid bouncing checks by keeping good records?

  A successful entrepreneur must have a good handle on money at all times. Managing cash flow is quite different from anticipating a weekly paycheck from an employer.

While considering your responses to this questionnaire, think about the traits cited by most successful entrepreneurs when asked to name their most important characteristic: self-confidence, high self-esteem, high energy level, ability to set and achieve long-term goals, persistence, drive style, motivation, ambition, ability to take initiative, ability to learn from mistakes, risk-taking, resourcefulness, creativity, and innovative style. What do you think? Do many of these terms describe you? If so, then you're on your way to actuating your goal!

3
Planning

Business Organization

Nearly all home-based secretarial services businesses are sole proprietorships (as compared with the two other most common forms of business organization: partnership and corporation). I have been a sole proprietor from day one and have never had any reason to change; however, I'll briefly discuss these three types of business ownership and outline the pros and cons.

Sole Proprietorship

Being a sole proprietor means exactly that—working by yourself, for yourself. You can simply hang out a shingle, once you've obtained the necessary permits. No attorney is needed for structuring complex partnership agreements or laws of incorporation; nor is an accountant absolutely required for filing your tax return (you fill out a one-page Schedule C and attach it to your federal income tax return). There may, however, be a number of areas in which you believe professional advice from both accounting and legal professionals would be of value, and if so, you are encouraged to pursue this avenue. Still, your costs are significantly reduced as a result of not *requiring* these services at the onset of establishing your business. Other advantages to sole proprietorships over other forms of business organization include the following: You are the sole "boss," with ultimate authority and responsibility, and there are potentially significant income tax advantages to being a sole proprietor who is home-based. Disadvantages include some of the more obvious items, such as the following: You have full exposure and unlimited liability in the event of a legal suit (highly unlikely); if you were to become seriously ill or die, your business activities would cease; and a home-based business structured as a sole proprietorship is limited, in terms of expansion and growth, by your ability to work.

Partnership

Most partnership arrangements have the benefit of a legal agreement between parties (although this can be an oral agreement, that method is not recommended). Agreements are necessary to provide for disposition of assets in the event that one or both parties wish to disconnect from the business at some future point. There are greater costs in entering a partnership as compared with a sole proprietorship, from both an accounting and a legal standpoint. Advantages to this method of business organization include having a partner with whom to consult and pool resources and ideas (financial and creative) and having someone with whom to share the problems. Disadvantages beyond added costs include difficulty in determining a compatible partner with whom you can establish clear working guidelines and a division of workload and managerial responsibility, blurring of managerial control over the business, difficulty encountered if the partnership doesn't work out, potential loss of friendship if the partner is a friend (worse if the partner is a family member), and lifespan of the business in the event of the partner's death.

Corporation

The most expensive way to begin a business also brings with it an advantage the two other forms of organization don't: limited liability (not necessarily the case for small business, however). Establishing a corporation will require legal and accounting fees, but this method of business organization generally allows for greater ease in raising capital for your business and provides for continuity in the event of your death. Disadvantages include higher taxes, restricted ability to "act like an entrepreneur" (depending on the covenants and restrictions of your charter and the board of directors), and perhaps a false sense of security.

While your own advisers should guide you, I highly recommend beginning as a sole proprietor. For nearly every home-based business in this field, a sole proprietorship is the most popular form of business organization. It's the least expensive way to run a business, requires the simplest and easiest-to-keep set of books and records, and is practical. Keep in mind that even as a sole proprietor, you do have the ability to have subcontracted freelance people handle work for you and even to have employees (the former is preferred; more on this later).

The next two aspects of planning—assessment of your competition and selection of your business name—should occur before spending considerable time developing a business plan.

Researching and Assessing the Competition

At this point it makes good business sense to find out who the competition is. It's unlikely that you're the first person to consider offering these types of services in your area. Find out who're out there, what they're doing, and how long they've been in business. Find out what they charge and if they're home-based. Try to determine their clientele profile and the niche they service. See where you can fit in—be more competitive pricewise starting out, perhaps, or offer a better-quality product, or offer a version of a service not currently available.

How do you do this? Obviously, the library does not provide copies of your competitors' business plans and sales records. Nor is this information likely to come easily by simple telephone inquiry. To gain information about your competition requires a little creativity and some solid market research. Start with your town's telephone directory, consulting all Yellow Pages listings under such categories as Copying, Desktop Publishing, Editing, Facsimile Transmission Service, Notary Public, Office Services, Photocopying, Proofreading, Resumes, Secretarial Service, Transcription, Typesetting, Typing Service, Word Processing Service, and any other category where services you're interested in providing might be listed.

Next, through either the library or an office of the local telephone company, obtain directories for all neighboring communities and repeat the process. Finally, check with your chamber of commerce for a membership listing (also a good networking source for prospective clients).

With these data in hand, use the following Assessment of the Competition Worksheet to develop your data analysis of the competition. Develop a separate set of worksheets for *each* business area in which you are interested (i.e., group all information gleaned about those businesses providing typing services together, group separately those companies providing resume services, etc.).

Once you've collected these data for each directory and in each category, use the following Advertised Categories Worksheet to tabulate your findings. This will form the backbone of your research into the competition. Keep in mind too that if older telephone directories and listings are available, you should compare these data with those of the previous year or years. Doing so will help to illustrate who is new to the industry (at least from the standpoint of advertising), who has dropped out from a prior year, and who has been around for a while. This last category—businesses that have been in existence for longer than just a few years—represents the prime target area about which you really want to obtain information around pricing and services offered.

Assessment of the Competition Worksheet

Directory for City/Town of ___Mapleville___

Category ___Typing Service___

Total Number of Companies Listed under this Category ___6___

Company Name	Town	✓*	Telephone	Services Provided	Size Ad**
A Good Word	Mapleville	✓	555-0001	laser documents, corresp., theses	2" in-column
Business Pros	Mapleton		555-0002	not itemized	Bold listing
Data Documents	Mapleville		555-0003	"	Single line
Debbie's Sec. Svs.	"	✓	555-0004	FAX, typesetting, laser, business svc.	1.5" in-column
Typing Techs	"		555-0005	Word Processing	bold listing & line
Word Wizards	Maple City		555-0006	Copies - FAX complete sec. svs.	3" in-column

* Check if you know or suspect the business is home-based; a good "giveaway" is if no address is published (or only a P.O. box is provided).

** For in-column ads this would be the depth of the ad in inches. For display ads size is computed using width and height so that a 2 X 4 ad is two columns wide by 4 inches deep. Also note if there is no ad but simply a single line listing, a boldface/caps listing, or a reference to see an ad elsewhere in the book.

Assessment of the Competition Worksheet

Directory for City/Town of _____

Category _____

Total Number of Companies Listed under this Category _____

Company Name	Town	✓ *	Telephone	Services Provided	Size Ad **

* Check if you know or suspect the business is home-based; a good "giveaway" is if no address is published (or only a P.O. box is provided).

** For in-column ads this would be the depth of the ad in inches. For display ads size is computed using width and height so that a 2 X 4 ad is two columns wide by 4 inches deep. Also note if there is no ad but simply a single line listing, a boldface/caps listing, or a reference to see an ad elsewhere in the book.

Advertised Categories Worksheet

City/Town Directory for **Mapleville**

Substitute headings from your area's directories; these are just examples. Using the data collected in the previous exercise, enter each company's name under all of the categories under which they advertise. You should begin to see some patterns develop and be able to recognize the "heavy hitters" in your geographic area, that is, the companies that are the most heavily advertised. In all likelihood, they are the businesses that are the most successful.

Desktop Publishing	Resumes	Secretarial Service	Typing Service	Word Processing Service	Multiple Listers
ABC Press	ABC Press				2
Business Pros			Business Pros		2
Fran's DTP					
Typing Techs		Typing Techs	Typing Techs		3
Word Wizards	Word Wizards	Word Wizards	Word Wizards	Word Wizards	5
	Business Res.				
	Career Dev. Pros.				
		Sec'y Svs. Plus			
		Typing Svs., Inc.		Typing Svs., Inc.	2
		Yolando's Svs.			
			A Good Word		
			Data Docum.	Data Docum.	2
			Debbie's Ser. Bus.		
				Alladin's Bus. Svs.	
				Imaginings Words	
TOTALS					
5	4	5	6	5	6

Advertised Categories Worksheet

City/Town Directory for _____

Substitute headings from your area's directories. Using the data collected in the previous exercise, enter each company's name under all of the categories under which they advertise. You should begin to see some patterns develop and be able to recognize the "heavy hitters" in your geographic area, that is, the companies that are the most heavily advertised. In all likelihood, they are the businesses that are the most successful.

Desktop Publishing	Resumes	Secretarial Service	Typing Service	Word Processing Service	Multiple Listers
TOTALS					

You should also repeat this exercise at the time of year each telephone directory is published for your area. This will keep you up to date on who your competition continues to be and will allow you to spot trends quickly (e.g., if in your area there is a trend toward using the color red in ads or if everyone in the business is going from an in-column to a display ad, you may want to follow suit; more information on this topic is available under Yellow Pages Advertising in chapter 4).

Now, armed with the results of your excellent research, it's time to begin the real analysis. One common way to obtain information about your competition is to contact them directly. Place telephone calls to competitors to inquire about getting a resume typed (if that's a service you are thinking of offering). You might wish to say you are calling for information for your spouse/friend if you'd rather not state your name. Call another day and inquire about having a term paper typed (again, if this is an area that interests you). Be sure to have your question checklist ready: What equipment is used? a laser printer? Do you charge per page? per hour? What about corrections? How many copies are included? What type of paper is used, what is the charge per sheet? Enlist a friend/spouse to assist with placing the calls if you feel uncomfortable making them. Ask about the experience of the individual you talk with, that is, how long the operation has been in business. If you think you may be speaking with a home-based secretarial service owner, ask if you are calling a home office. Record on your worksheets all information obtained—and retain this information. It will be useful when you "test the market" each year to determine where the competition is heading in terms of the services provided and the costs charged.

Another valuable way to conduct research and gain extensive knowledge is to contact businesses outside of your market area, perhaps in another area of your state where you represent no threat. Ask to speak with the owner and identify yourself, indicating that you are beginning your own word processing service (or whatever you've decided to offer). Immediately mention that you deliberately selected this company to call because it's not in the area and therefore you are not a competitive threat whatsoever.

Ask if the owner would be willing to spend a few minutes (hopefully, more) with you on the telephone to answer a few questions—if not then, perhaps at another, scheduled time. Ideally, the person you'll be talking with once started his or her own company (perhaps initially home-based, or still home-based) and knows what you're going through. With that type of empathy, you could obtain very useful information. The person might even be willing to meet with you in his or her office for an hour or two. If so, take advantage of it, and if you hit "pay dirt" and acquire some great information, remember to acknowledge it professionally and promptly with a thank-you note.

You might try calling your local competition and asking them "how to get started." But as nice as people are, that generally is ineffective. Just jumping out of your local telephone dialing area should be adequate and well worth the toll charges on your telephone bill.

Selection of Your Business Name

Now you're ready for the *fun* part—selecting a name for your firm. This is also very serious business because once you've selected your name and gone to the expense of creating all your business materials using that name (and then developing name recognition among your clients and in your geographic area), you won't casually want to change it. So give this exercise a great deal of thought. If you're like many would-be entrepreneurs, you probably have some ideas in mind and may already have designed some preliminary logos and even slogans for your stationery. If so, take a close look at the suggestions provided to see if most of these criteria have been incorporated in your selection process. If you haven't given extensive thought to determining your company's name, here are some recommendations to get you started.

Many business owners, secretarial services included, opt to use their own name and call themselves something like "Jane Brown Associates." Depending on how your telephone directory lists names, this could be fine, because many will show the listing as

"Brown, Jane," followed by "Jane Brown Associates" in the actual ad copy. This is good—because placement within the alphabet can be key! Unfortunately most of the business words you might readily think of tend to start with letters that are not located near the beginning of the alphabet—*professional, secretarial, typing, service, word processing*—as do many of the clever catch phrases used in our industry: Letter Perfect, Wordsmith, Ways with Words, Typing Pros. Don't let that stop you from becoming creative. If your name doesn't lend itself to good placement alphabetically, begin experimenting.

I recommend staying away from the obvious AAA Services or Aardvark Systems, employed solely for alphabetical placement. If you're not using your own name or initials, attempt to select a name that will describe some element of the business services you intend to provide, yet be as expansive as possible. I know of people in this business choosing to name their service something like Quick Typing Service ten years ago, then updating it to Quick Word Processing Service five years later, when word processing nearly replaced typing from a technological standpoint. Now a change to Quick Desktop Publishing Services is being considered. Who knows where technological advancements will take this field in the next five to ten years? For that reason a less focused approach might be better with regard to name selection.

Getting back to alphabetical placement, why is this so all important? Because how you are listed in the Yellow Pages of the telephone directory (or directories) in which you will appear is *critical* and can't be stressed enough. Even clients who know you and your company name will frequently use the Yellow Pages to look you up in order to call . . . and prospective clients that need a service and don't know who to call will start at the top of the heading they're looking under (say, Secretarial Service) and work their way down.

Once you've selected a name, experiment with it. Try out various styles and fonts. See how it looks on drafts of a letterhead or business card, or a mock-up of a Yellow Pages ad. Ask opinions of others. Then wait a few days. If you still love it when you go back to it a week later, go with it. Finally, refer to the section on Legal Technicalities and Zoning Issues to Consider in chapter 1 for information about properly recording your name with local and state agencies.

Developing a Complete Business Plan

Don't let this scare you. Development of a business plan for your secretarial service can be as simple and uncomplicated (or as complex) as you choose. This section presents a description of the basic components of a business plan to which you will need to give consideration. A business plan is really nothing more than a road map of how you intend to start, develop, and operate your business, with an eye to the future. A business plan is essential if you are seeking funds from a lending institution. But it's a good idea to have a business plan even if you are not seeking any loans, because developing the plan will help you to focus on all the necessary aspects of properly planning your business for success. Once developed, a good business plan will allow you to evaluate your business periodically as well as monitor sales growth and profitability.

The following sections should be components of your business plan (some categories require only a few lines or a paragraph).

Executive Summary

Although placed at the front of the business plan, this is generally written last, after you've pulled together all the other pieces of your plan. This should stress the most important sections of your business plan clearly and succinctly. Information typically included would be your name, the business name, the location of the business, the services you intend to provide, the market niches you intend to serve, the rationale for starting your business (i.e., why you are able to offer a "better mousetrap" than the competition), and—if you are seeking financing from a lending institution—the amount you are requesting and your plans for disbursement.

General Description of Business

Here you repeat the above information and also mention your form of business organization (usually sole proprietorship). If you've already started your business, indicate the actual date commenced. Describe in detail the types of services you will provide and the intended clients. For example, you might indicate that because you are located within 10 miles of four colleges and universities, you intend to develop a strong market niche providing services to students (term papers, theses, doctoral dissertations, and resumes/cover letters upon graduation).

Also included in this section would be information about the planned financial status of the business. If you haven't actually started the business, you would provide projections based on your anticipated charges (see Establishing a Price Structure in chapter 5). Using the example above of providing services to students, you might indicate that your hourly rate will be $24, that you anticipate fifteen billable hours per week (on average) in your first year of business, and that you plan on working 50 weeks in the first year and therefore project revenues of $18,000.

A final segment in this section includes your short- and long-term goals for the business. In continuing the example provided above, you might present as your short-term goal fully developing the niche servicing students in your first year. In year 2 your goal might be to average twenty-five billable hours per week, with an increase in your rates to $26 per hour and three weeks' vacation (thereby working forty-nine weeks). This would project annual revenues at nearly $32,000. For a longer-term goal you might project expanding your services to include professional word processing and transcription services for the business community that supports the neighboring universities. For year 5 you might project implementing a two-tiered price schedule, having thirty billable hours per week at a rate of $35 and five billable hours per week at a rate of $45 (editorial/transcription). You might also project four weeks' vacation (working 48 weeks). This yields $61,200 per year in gross annual revenues. Included in your long-term planning might also be speculation of hiring part- or full-time assistance, either as freelance, subcontracted typing help or perhaps as a part-time, in-office person to cover telephones, handle filing and copying, and so forth.

(*Note:* These numbers are purely hypothetical and not necessarily representative of the norm in your geographic area.)

Products and Services

This component of a business plan is where you would describe your physical setting (outline the basic furniture and room in your home that will be devoted to the business). Mention procurement of local permits for the business. Examples of your work could be included (e.g., a formatted resume or a brochure or newsletter). A complete listing of the services your business will provide should be included, accompanied by typical charges. For example, if you plan to handle resumes, you will probably want to establish different pricing for different levels of service—simply typing a client's handwritten, one-page resume might have a flat charge of $25, whereas meeting with a client, conducting a consultation, then writing "from scratch" a one-page resume would naturally cost more, perhaps $75 or $100. If you plan to handle document preparation, such as theses or reports, you might show what your hourly rate is and then give an estimated per page rate (for instance, if your hourly rate is $20 and you follow the industry standard of producing approximately eight double-spaced pages per hour, you would quote about $2.50 per page).

This section regarding products and services should also discuss the advantages of doing business with you. What unique attributes do you offer? You might mention your professional experience before beginning your own company or discuss your educational background, either in learning the various skills required of an excellent secretary or in earning a business degree. You would also mention specialized services you can provide. Are you bilingual? Do you offer translation services as well? Can you take shorthand in addition to providing transcription? Will you provide pickup and delivery services? Do you plan to offer rush, overnight, or even same-day service (for an uplifted charge)? These are all business attributes to mention.

Market and Industry Data

This is where your hard work collecting competitive research information comes in handy. Merely compile the statistics you collected about your competition and their service offerings and pricing and rank them against your planned services and fees. It will probably be impossible for you to know or calculate market share by your competitors (as might be done by a cosmetics giant in launching a new line of skin care products), but you may be able to compare your geographic proximity to the intended clientele with that of your competitors and cite again the unique attributes you will offer.

Marketing Strategy

There is substantial information on this topic in chapter 4. You'll want to review it, certainly, before including information in your business plan. Basically, you should outline how you plan to acquire clients. Using our student example, this could include placing flyers under the windshield wipers of cars in student parking lots; posting flyers throughout campus buildings and classrooms; advertising in university newsletters, university telephone directories, and regular telephone company Yellow Pages; using direct mail (to department heads); and perhaps providing discount or repeat client offers or coupons toward future services. You might structure a student discount price for cash in advance. All these items would be mentioned.

Operational Plan

This section describes the equipment you will use in your secretarial services business. There is an outline to which you can refer later in this chapter. If you haven't purchased equipment yet, you would include in the operational plan the anticipated cost of equipment, software, and supplies. Include anticipated vendors you will be using (consult the Appendix for recommended supply vendors, in addition to your own local sources). If you are starting out your business as the only employee (the most common way to begin), you will be handling all the work. Describe your skills briefly.

Management "Team" and Organization

Once again, if you are starting out as the only employee, you'll be wearing all those hats described in chapter 2. Include in this section a brief summation of those various responsibilities.

Financial Plan

This, for many, represents the most difficult part in developing a business plan. Forms are provided in this chapter for you to use in compiling and calculating the appropriate information.

Appendix

In addition to attaching your business card, brochure, and/or newsletter (if you have developed any of these pieces) to your business plan, you should also attach your resume and any letters of reference (these could include letters from past employers as well as clients). If you have received any publicity in local newspapers (you will; more on this in chapter 4), include copies with your business plan.

Expense Worksheet

You will probably find that you do not have as expenses some of the items listed on the Expense Worksheet Form for your business, particularly in the start-up phase. This worksheet should be completed after the close of each month to maintain an accurate picture of the financial health of your business.

Balance Sheet

From an accounting standpoint, a balance sheet is simply a "snapshot" in time at any given point of the overall financial health of your company. It represents a summary of your assets, liabilities, and net worth. The numbers on a balance sheet must "tie"; that is, your assets minus your liabilities equal capital or net worth. A brief definition of each of the categories on a balance sheet follows.

Current assets—whatever your business has of value that can be converted to cash within a short period of time (under a year). This includes cash in your business checking and savings accounts and in your petty cash fund, as well as equipment, office supplies, and accounts receivables.

Projecting Start-up Costs Worksheet

Fixtures and equipment (information in chapter 3)	$ _____
Remodeling, renovation, and decorating expense	$ _____
Installation of equipment	$ _____
Deposit to telephone company	$ _____
Cost of business telephone line	$ _____
Legal and professional fees	$ _____
Licenses and permits	$ _____
Business insurance for a home-based business	$ _____
Starting inventory of office supplies/stationery	$ _____
Initial advertising/promotion costs	$ _____
Operating cash	$ _____
Miscellaneous	$ _____
TOTAL	$ _____

Sample Start-up Office Supply Inventory

20-pound paper suitable for both laser printer and ...... 1 case (10 reams)
copier (cheaper by the case and you will use it;
buy 24 pound if you can afford it)

manila file folders .... box of 100

8½ x 11 writing tablets .... package of 12

oversize envelopes (9 x 12) .... box of 100

#10 business envelopes (white) .... box of 500

small pads for telephone messages 6

Post-It™ notes (2-inch-square size) .... small package

paper clips .... 1 box

stapler with staples .... 1 box staples

pica stick and ruler .... 1 each

scissors .... 1 pair

rubber cement and Elmer's glue .... 1 each

cellophane tape with dispenser .... 2 rolls

self-inking stamp: "First Class" 1

first-class postage stamps .... roll of 100

extra incremental ounce postage stamps .... sheet of 100

small postage scale 1

small desktop calculator (portable is ideal) 1

disks appropriately sized for your computer .... 3 boxes (10 per box)

pens (blue or black ink) .... box of 10

pencils .... box of 10

fine-point black ink pens 2

highlighting markers .... 4 different colors, 1 each

labels suitable for use in laser printer or copier .... box of 100 sheets

If you opt not to have preprinted letterhead and envelopes, be certain to have an appropriate quantity of your preferred stock and matching envelopes in storage for printing your own as you need them. Invoice forms are typically printed individually as you generate billing on your computer and therefore do not require preprinted forms.

Optional (depending on if you will be offering resume services; this would be the minimum start-up inventory for this service)

24-pound ivory parchment .... 3 boxes (100 sheets each)

matching envelopes .... 4 boxes (25 to a box)

24-pound ice blue or stone gray parchment ...... 3 boxes (100 sheets each)

matching envelopes .... 4 boxes (25 to a box)

24-pound pure white parchment .... 2 boxes (100 sheets each)

matching envelopes .... 3 boxes (25 to a box)

Fixed assets—your equipment investments and office furniture, minus depreciation.

Liabilities—the unpaid expenses of the business for which you are responsible. These include your business telephone bill, any maintenance contract costs, office supply bills, and so on. Also included would be any debts you incurred to start your business, such as bank or personal loans.

Capital (also known as equity or net worth)—the number resulting when you subtract your liabilities from your assets.

Profit and Loss Statement

This is also referred to as an income statement and should ideally be prepared monthly or quarterly, but some companies prepare them just once per year. This is another important document that can be used to assess the economic health of your business.

Cash Flow Projections

The final form included in your business plan represents a month-to-month comparison between estimated and actual income and expenses (and should be updated on a monthly basis). In any start-up business you will naturally have more cash "outgo" than income. This reinforces the reason for having a solid savings base on which to draw for at least the first six months of your business. Many start-up secretarial service owners pay themselves no salary for the first few months or even year in business. Instead, they constantly reinvest any profits in the beginning to further develop their business, adding to their promotional and marketing efforts and the like.

See chapter 5's recommendations under Recordkeeping for techniques in establishing your business records as well as creating sales analysis documents by client and by profit center to truly help you manage your business growth. All of these documents can be easily prepared in either a word processing program on your computer or in a spreadsheet program, such as Excel or Lotus. There are numerous software accounting packages available as well; two of my favorites (in the Macintosh world) are Quicken and Dollars + Sense.

Expense Worksheet Form

Month/Year _____

Salary	$ _____
Payment on note/business loan	$ _____
Equipment lease costs	$ _____
Telephone	$ _____
Yellow Pages advertising (usually itemized separately on telephone bill)	$ _____
Other advertising	$ _____
Fax telephone charges	$ _____
Office supplies	$ _____
Printing costs (business stationery)	$ _____
Stationery and supplies	$ _____
Postage	$ _____
Bank service charges	$ _____
Federal Express/other delivery charges	$ _____
Professional dues	$ _____
Professional subscriptions	$ _____
Taxes and licenses	$ _____
Insurance	$ _____
Travel and entertainment	$ _____
Medical insurance	$ _____
Mileage and parking expenses	$ _____
Maintenance contract costs (computer, copier, fax, etc.)	$ _____
Repairs and maintenance expense	$ _____
"Rent"/contribution to utilities	$ _____
Security system/monitoring expense	$ _____
Office cleaning expense	$ _____
Freelance subcontractors	$ _____
Courier service	$ _____
Miscellaneous	$ _____

Balance Sheet Form

FOR _____(name of your company)_____

AS OF _____(specific date)_____

ASSETS

Current Assets/Cash:

Cash in bank	$ ———————
Petty cash	$ ———————
Accounts receivable	$ ———————
Supply inventories	$ ———————
Total Current Assets	$ ———————

Fixed Assets:

Office furnishings	$ ———————
Office equipment	$ ———————
Less allowance for depreciation	$ ———————
Total Fixed Assets	$ ———————
TOTAL ASSETS	$ ———————

LIABILITIES AND CAPITAL

Current Liabilities:

Accounts payable	$ ———————
Notes payable, due within 1 year	$ ———————
Sales taxes	$ ———————
Quarterly taxes	$ ———————
Total Current Liabilities	$ ———————

Long-term Liabilities:

Notes payable, due after 1 year	$ ———————
TOTAL LIABILITIES	$ ———————

Capital:

Proprietor's capital, beginning of period	$ ———————
Net profit for the period	$ ———————
Less proprietor's draw (salary)	$ ———————
Increase in capital	$ ———————
Capital, end of period	$ ———————
TOTAL LIABILITIES AND CAPITAL	$ ———————

Profit and Loss Statement Form

FOR _____ (name of your company) _____

FOR THE MONTH (OR YEAR) _____

GROSS SALES	$ _____
COST OF SALES:	
Opening inventory/supplies on hand	$ _____
Purchases	_____
Total	_____
Ending inventory	_____
TOTAL COST OF SALES	_____

GROSS PROFIT		
OPERATING EXPENSES:		
"Rent"/contribution to utilities	_____	
Loan payments	_____	
Depreciation	_____	
Mileage/parking costs	_____	
Telephone and advertising	_____	
Office supplies/printing costs	_____	
Postage	_____	
Fax expenses	_____	
Bank service charges	_____	
Dues/subscriptions	_____	
Delivery and courier expenses	_____	
Maintenance contract costs/repairs	_____	
Office cleaning expense	_____	
Security system	_____	
Travel and entertainment	_____	
Medical/office insurance	_____	
Taxes and licenses	_____	
Freelance subcontractors	_____	
Miscellaneous	_____	
TOTAL		_____
NET PROFIT [before your salary]		$ _____

Cash Flow Projections Form

FOR _____(name of your company)_____

FOR THE MONTH _____

	Estimate	Actual
1. Cash on hand (at start of month)		
2. a. Cash receipts		
b. Loan receipts/injection of $ into business		
3. TOTAL CASH AVAILABLE (1+2.a.+2.b.)		
4. Cash paid out		
a. Salary		
b. Taxes/licenses		
c. Office supplies/printing/postage		
d. Delivery services/courier		
e. Office/medical insurance		
f. Telephone/fax/advertising		
g. Other advertising		
h. "Rent"/contribution to utilities		
i. Mileage/parking		
j. Professional dues/subscriptions		
k. Legal and professional fees		
l. Maintenance service contracts/repairs		
m. Loan payments/interest		
n. Bank service charges		
o. Travel and entertainment		
p. Office cleaning/security system		
q. Freelance subcontractors		
r. Equipment purchases/leases		
s. Miscellaneous		
t. SUBTOTAL (4.a. through 4.s.)		
u. Any of your withdrawals		
5. TOTAL CASH PAID OUT (4.t.+4.u.)		
6. End-of-month cash position (3–5)		
Non-cash-flow operating information for the month		
• Sales volume in dollars		
• Accounts receivables at month's end		
• Dollar value of inventory/supplies at month's end		
• Accounts payable at month's end		
• Depreciation		

Capital Equipment Acquisition

While some individuals operate a "typing" business with just a typewriter, most clients will expect at least basic word processing capability; many will want and gladly pay for additional services, including desktop publishing, laser printing, and photocopying, as well as fax and notary public services.

A significant advantage to starting this type of business is that you can begin small and build as your client base and revenues grow. Plus, there are generally significant tax advantages and legitimate write-offs the first few years of beginning and operating a business.

The following lists detail suggested basic equipment as well as recommended add-on equipment to enhance your services. Expanding your service offerings with the additional equipment will increase your earnings potential as your client base broadens. The timeframe in which to add equipment can be determined by you as funds are available, as your earnings increase, and so on. Some services never offer all of the enhanced services; others start out offering "everything" from day one. Most home-based businesses find they successfully and reasonably add to their service offerings on a gradual basis, stretching out their acquisitions over several years' time. That's the flexibility you have as a business owner.

Estimates vary substantially based on geographic area, brands, and so forth. Also, don't overlook "gently used" equipment (see Highly Recommended Tip later in this section).

Basic Start-up Equipment

- computer system (ideally, with a full-page monitor) $1,000–$4,500

- word processing software/spreadsheet software (see information below regarding recommended minimum features) $300–$500 ea.

- laser printer (necessary for resume work or handling corporate clients' material) or ink jet/letter-quality printer (if laser printer cost is prohibitive) $750–$3,000

- electric or electronic typewriter (you'll need this for completing school, grant, and employment applications) $175–$350

- business telephone and line (separate from *phone set* residence telephone line; a phone set with *monthly base* that includes both your residence line and your business line is ideal, in particular, if you have the "hold" button feature—perfect when children interrupt you when you're speaking with a client; you can place your caller "on hold" like a "real" office) $25–$150+ $20–$40

- answering machine for business telephone $45+

Highly Recommended Tip

An answering machine with a *portable phone* is a wonderful aid in being able to handle myriad responsibilities—from filing "silently" while on a lengthy call with a client who likes to chat and throwing dinner (quietly) into the oven, to tossing laundry into the dryer or checking on a napping baby, all while conducting business over the phone. It's well worth the $150 or so. It also will enable you to work outdoors and not miss business calls, if you so choose (especially nice when weather allows and you have a lengthy proofreading project).

Recommended Basic Features for Word Processing Software Program

- Ability to open more than one document at a time

- Ability to search and replace text within a document using one command or simply search for specific text

- Ability to bold, underline, italicize, expand, condense, outline, shadow, type all caps, type small caps, undo all caps

- Ability to key information into header and footer menus, including separate menus for "first header" and/or "first footer"

- Well-designed margin feature that provides for automatic tabbing as well as a number of margin settings, including left and right (flush left and flush right), justified, centered, decimal tabbing, word wrapping
- Ability to scale font sizes easily in 1-point increments
- Features for indexing and footnoting functions
- Ability to set and reset page numbers at will
- Ability to set text leading and key single, single plus a half, or double spacing
- Ability to set superscript and subscript in 1-point increments
- Ability to conduct automatic hyphenation and word counting
- Ability to set page layout to portrait or landscape
- Ability to select word, paragraph, and document segments easily
- Ability to set margins to exact sizes (all four sides of page)
- Ability to set "smart quotes"
- Ability to spellcheck and create unique dictionaries
- Ability to consult thesaurus
- Ability to create a data document, then set up a mail merge easily
- Ability to apply borders and shading to sections of text
- Multiple column capability

Furniture

- solid work space/desk with an area of the proper height for your monitor and keyboard $75+

- good quality, ergonomically designed chair (the best you can afford—you'll be "living" in this chair!) $125–$300+

- small file cabinet for client records and files (temporary cardboard files that stack are a satisfactory alternative) $25–$75

- area devoted to storage supplies (free from humidity and the curious fingers of young children; a shelf or two in your probably already crowded linen closet is fine—but not in the bathroom: too much humidity, which is not good for paper supplies); keep in mind too that if you have young children, you don't want them to be able to access such supplies as correction fluid, markers, and toner cartridges, which contain chemicals and could pose health problems if ingested. Safety is paramount! $ 0

Other Start-up Costs

- professionally prepared business cards (see details under Business Cards in chapter 4) $25–$100+

- business checking account (a d/b/a account— "Susan Smith doing business as Wordsmith Associates") and first order of checks; a d/b/a account is the most common way to establish a business account as a sole proprietor. $30+

- basic stationery/office supplies (see Proposed Start-up Office Supply Inventory); your best buys will undoubtedly be through bulk office supply warehouses and discount mail firms (see the Appendix for suggested mail-order vendors); however, it's strongly suggested that you establish and cultivate a good relationship with a local printer and an office supply store—they consistently stock the same brands, unlike the warehouse; are convenient for last-minute, rush merchandise (usually offering delivery); and are an excellent source of new client referrals. $75–$300

- maintenance service contracts on equipment during post warranty years   *varies* $100/yr.+

- business insurance policy that not only protects you from liability in the event of personal injury but offers protection for theft, fire, and damage to your office furnishings, equipment, etc. This is an important expense frequently overlooked by start-up secretarial service owners.

varies significantly from a $6.00 annual rider on your regular homeowner's policy to $250–$350 for a business policy. Shop around!

- discreet, professional, attractive business sign for your driveway/home (be sure it's in compliance with local zoning regulations)

$75–$300

- advertising (see chapter 4)

varies

Highly Recommended Tip

Purchase high-quality *used* office furniture. Save your investment dollars for early advertising and expensive computer equipment and software. Scout out quality used office furniture and equipment stores in your area, often the nearest large town. You might also check with large companies in your locale that might be moving and be interested in selling their used equipment. Look for top-quality brands (such as Steelcase) and excellent serviceability; don't worry about appearance—yet. You should be able to find a good used desk for under $100, a used vertical four-drawer file cabinet for under $50, and a good used chair for under $75 (prices vary depending on your geographic area; check around and you'll become an expert on what to pay for used office furniture). Foreclosure and auction sales can also yield great buys.

If you've managed to piece together used equipment from various sources—used furniture stores, tag sales, basements, and so on—give consideration to having a professional office furniture refinishing company electrostatically repaint all of the metal portions of your furniture and equipment to match. If you've saved hundreds of dollars through carefully selected quality used merchandise, you might feel comfortable justifying the cost of this repainting (especially if the furniture is otherwise in good condition—just scratched, marred, and unmatching, e.g., a black desk, a brown file cabinet, and a putty tan typing stand). The cost of such repainting is usually under $500.

I assisted with organizing a sale of used office furniture for my full-time employer back when I began my own company. As was the case with all of my colleagues helping out, we were able to have "first pick" of the used goods at great prices. I purchased a 6-foot mahogany-look conference table, a single pedestal desk with a return (for my computer), three upholstered chairs on wheels, a large credenza, two bookcases, and a four-drawer file cabinet—all for under $100. I had every color in the business furniture rainbow represented, however—black, tan, beige, putty, and gray! But the quality was excellent, and there was virtually no damage or wear. The following spring I had all of the colored surfaces electrostatically refinished in a gorgeous burgundy color that beautifully picks up a color in the wallpaper of my office. I coordinated the deep forest green background of the wallpaper with a thick pile carpet of the same shade bearing maroon flecks—so I'm completely "decorated," all on a shoestring! Best of all, even the refinishing of my furniture was a bargain: In my state's annual public television auction, I was the successful bidder on a refinishing package. The item was auctioned at 12:30 A.M. and, because I'm a night owl, I was practically the only bidder as well as the successful one. I got the $500 package for a mere $220! And the company handled all of the painting right in my office. No one would ever guess that my furniture didn't start out as a coordinated set.

Highly Recommended Tip

Purchase your computer system and/or peripherals from a student at a local university. Stretch your investment dollars to cover a system maintenance contract (strongly advised) and additional software. If you live anywhere near a large university or college, chances are good that there are students eager to trade up their computer equipment and seeking to do so through an outside sale in the community. This is a great means by which to get good value for your money. Watch local newspapers for classified advertising under Computers. To most effectively take advantage of the bargains to be found in this market, you should ideally possess a good working knowledge of computers, have identified the type of system you want to own, and know something about the various operating systems, model numbers, and so forth. Also, computer magazines usually publish second-hand pricing to give you a negotiating point (e.g., *MacWorld* provides pricing for used Macs each month). Most students are more than willing to share their knowledge about their computer systems; many sell their equipment "as is"—thus giving you the added benefit of hundreds, even thousands of dollars of "free" software (already installed on the system), albeit usually without documentation. For documentation you'll be able to purchase guides from a large bookstore (a campus bookstore is ideal) that will help you with much of what might be included. Over time you'll eventually want to buy your own software, with upgrade privileges, complete documentation, registration, support resources, and the like. But this is a great way to start small and build up.

When I converted to the Macintosh at year 5 in my business cycle, I purchased my first and second Mac SEs exactly in this fashion from students at a nearby university (I watched for their newspaper ads). I successfully negotiated excellent purchase prices and never regretted getting into the "Mac world" in this way. As I've expanded my business, I've outgrown the need for my smaller Macs and sold them through my own newspaper ads in the same way.

Again, regardless of the manner in which you acquire your computer equipment, it is highly recommended that you place *all* of it under a maintenance contract or agreement. If you successfully negotiate a sale with a private party, be certain that your conditions of sale include a clause that provides you with a reasonable period of time in which to ensure that the system is inspected by a qualified computer maintenance organization and suitable for placement under a service agreement. If prearranged with a service company (and it should be), a twenty-four to forty-eight-hour period of time should be adequate, and most students are reasonable and will accept this as a condition of final sale.

Always be sure to have a copy of the bill of sale for your tax records. And be certain to obtain the telephone number and address of the party from which you buy your system—a good source of free troubleshooting support for as long as school is in session that year.

Other good sources of equipment include the large variety of publications specifically aimed at certain brands (there are magazines for the PC world, i.e., IBM and IBM-compatible, and for the Macintosh, the two most prevalent small business system types in the country). If you're not already "into" computers and decide to make this your point of entry, you'll probably find yourself aligned with either the Mac or the IBM (or one of its many clones). Depending on whom you talk with, you'll be heavily steered toward one or the other. The general finding is that graphics people, writers, and creative sorts tend to prefer the intuitive Mac, whereas true business types like IBM. My background with computers was with Digital— the other "biggie" out there—and I converted to, and *love,* the Macintosh. I've also used IBM systems successfully, but I keep returning to my Macs. With ongoing technological advances and good file exchange utilities, you can generally convert documents from one system type to another relatively easily.

Enhanced Equipment and Furnishings

- desktop publishing software program $300–$700

- modem $75+

- additional filing, cabinet, and storage space   *varies*

- bookcase $50+

- fax machine*—this is frequently considered a $450–$1,400+
start-up necessity. It's a good profit center *and* brings in additional word processing business. In the case of thermal paper machines, be sure to pay the extra cost to have a machine with an automatic document feeder (usually up to 15 pages) and an automatic paper cutter for incoming faxes. Plain paper fax machines still cost

* See next page.

substantially more than thermal paper machines. Keep in mind that you don't need to outlay additional monies for a separate line for the fax—most home-based businesses use their personal house telephone line for their fax (however, a dedicated fax line is a luxurious plus, one that I installed, finally, after ten years in business). While you can't deduct the base monthly charge of the personal telephone line on your tax return when it is used for the fax, you can keep track of the toll charges incurred when transmitting faxes and deduct these as legitimate business expenses. Be sure to check for the most current guidelines with regard to the ability to deduct any business expense.

- good quality photocopier *—almost a necessity, $1,800–$2,500 but this can be deferred at start-up if you can't swing the financing (remember, though, that producing copies of text, reports, resumes, etc. represents an excellent profit generator).

* For both the fax machine and the photocopier, most companies offer lease packages, many with an option to purchase the equipment at the end of the lease. Although you end up paying more for the machine, you can own it at the end of the term and finance it in smaller increments as you grow your business. For some this is an excellent option. Check too with your accountant regarding the potential tax benefits to leasing versus buying your equipment.

4

Advertising and Promotion

As the owner of a secretarial services business, you are your own best public relations person. As a goodwill ambassador for your company, you have the opportunity to promote yourself and your services every time you speak with someone—friend, neighbor, local businessperson, and so on. Some of this speaking might be directly promotion-oriented; the majority will be subtle.

What types of clients do you wish to attract? (Keep in mind that you are providing a service to your *clients;* never make the mistake of calling them customers.) What niche are you hoping to fill? Gear your marketing, promotional, and advertising efforts accordingly.

Business Cards

Business cards will no doubt be your first business expense after arranging for installation of a business telephone line. Be certain *not* to order your cards until the telephone line is actually installed. In some infrequent instances the number does change from the one the telephone company may have originally promised you. You don't want to go through the expense of having your business cards reprinted simply because of an incorrect telephone number.

Basic information you'll want to include on your business card includes your business name (see Selection of Your Business Name in chapter 3), *your* name, and the business telephone number. You should also select and use a title for yourself. In my years of doing business, I've observed that, as a rule, female entrepreneurs frequently choose not to use a title—or they might say "owner," "operator," or "proprietor." On the other hand, most male entrepreneurs use titles and nearly always call themselves "president." While perhaps awkward to some at first, this *is* your company, and, male or female, you are certainly entitled to call yourself president, even if your business is not incorporated. Place your title right after your name on your business cards and on all other written materials where your name appears (e.g., letterhead).

If, like most home-based business owners, you do not wish to have drop-in clientele and prefer to schedule by appointment, I recommend omitting your physical street address and instead obtaining a post office box number—use that, plus your town, state, and zip code, on your business card. A quick summary of your key services should be included also, in particular if your business name doesn't describe what you do (e.g., "Allen Associates" is great for placement at the top of the alphabet but doesn't indicate what the company does). You should also include a "subhead" or a slogan beneath the company name that says something such as "Professional Word Processing and Typing Services."

If you offer multiple services, you might briefly itemize half a dozen or so in small, legible type. Try not to crowd too much onto one little card, but do be somewhat descriptive. Perhaps consider a two-sided business card or one with an overflap (both cost more, however). Play with the layout and text over and over again until you're satisfied with the look. I recommend typesetting the copy for your business cards using your own laser printer (if you have one) so that you can exactly match your letterhead and other business documents you will later be preparing on your equipment. Then let it "cool" for two days' time. Go back to it with fresh eyes and take another look. This is a step that's suggested every time you write copy for promotional and advertising purposes. Once it's finalized, you're ready to take it to a printer.

I used a standard-size business card for my first eight years in business but found that I was frequently asked at business meetings and conventions to jot down on the back of the card some of the specific services I provided. This began to become a nuisance, so I converted at that time to a double-size card with a folding flap. The card is distinctive and attracts positive attention, plus it enables me to detail some of the more specific services my company provides. I have found the cards to be well worth the cost (about $120 for 1,000 as compared with around $40 or $50 for standard-size cards of the same quantity).

Obtaining printing services for your business cards is a great opportunity to affiliate yourself with a professional printer in your area. Not only will you want to refer some business to that firm, but the printer will be pleased to know of your existence, and once you've proven yourself as a professional with "staying power," the printer will refer business to you that he or she doesn't handle (e.g., typesetting a resume). Call different vendors to obtain quotes for your business cards. The recommended start-up quantity is the minimum, usually 500. That way, as you expand services and equipment, your cards can be updated in a shorter amount of time with minimal waste of the outdated cards.

Go for the highest grade stock (paper) you can obtain. Crisp black ink on white linen vellum is tough to beat, in particular, because you can obtain a nice white stationery and reasonably priced envelopes instead of going with a much more costly colored stock that's difficult to obtain. You'll want a consistent, cohesive look to all of your printed materials—same type font, same stock (or similar stock but same color), and so on. Keep this in mind before deciding on "wild strawberry" as the color for your business cards! Choosing a pure white card stock costs less and, for businesses in the start-up phase, allows you to order inexpensive but professional-quality return labels, mailing labels, business-size envelopes with your return address, and so forth from such supply catalogs as Walter Drake and Spencer. If you pick an ivory or gray for your letterhead or business cards, for example, you won't be able to coordinate these other supplies as economically as when using white paper.

In addition, the availability of unique business stationery and forms for customized use in your laser printer (see the list of sources in the Appendix) allows for quick personalization of professional-looking brochures you write, design, and print yourself in quantities of one or more as needed.

If you've developed a logo, use it on your card as well as all other printed materials. If you've created a slogan, be sure to incorporate it also. Phrases like "THE Experts in Word Processing" and "The Resume Professionals" are catchy, quick, and memorable. Make sure your slogan reflects you.

Brochures

If you plan to be in the business of providing enhanced word processing or desktop publishing services, then you'll undoubtedly want to pursue the market for preparing brochures. The best way to capture this business? Develop your own eye-catching and professional brochure that showcases your talent and creativity! With the wide range of specialty papers available through such companies as Paper Direct (see the Appendix), you can stylize a unique, customized brochure and print only the quantity you need for a given promotional mailing. You'll be able to customize your message while at the same time tailoring services to the anticipated needs of certain client groups.

Also discuss with the printer you selected to handle your business cards the options and specialty papers available for large runs. While I always recommend against printing too many, particularly in the beginning, you may find it is more cost-effective to have 500 brochures produced on a distinctive paper carried by your printer.

What should a brochure include? Beyond the obvious information (name, address, telephone number, and, if you have one, fax number), you should detail *benefits* to your clients as well as services available. I am firmly of the opinion that you don't want

Established in 1983, Comprehensive Services Plus provides professional and creative services to clients in the Greater Middletown/Hartford and Boston areas. We're experts at helping your business develop materials that are action-oriented and capture the bottom-line results you're looking for.

■ ■ ■

We work closely with your staff to understand your strategic objectives and to implement effective, successful programs and materials — all while keeping a close watch on your budgetary constraints.

■ ■ ■

CSP also provides adjunct office services to relieve overload on your staff, produce timely leads follow-up, handle administrative overflow, and furnish essential secretarial assistance.

■ ■ ■

In short, whatever your particular requirements, you can rely on CSP to deliver the professional assistance you need in this challenging business climate. We help turn opportunities into realities!

■ ■ ■

Our Business Is
Making You Look Good!

COMPREHENSIVE SERVICES PLUS

P.O. Box 718
Durham, CT 06422
(203) 349-0256

Professional
Desktop Publishing,
Promotional, Editorial,
and Office Support Services

Since 1983

☎ **(203) 349-0256**
FAX **(203) 349-1343**

Providing the Professional Desktop Publishing, Promotional, Editorial, and Office Support Services Your Business Needs!

COMPREHENSIVE
SERVICES PLUS

From designing effective solutions to your communications problems to creating image-enhancing materials, our business is dedicated to helping *your* business be successful and competitive in today's marketplace. We can tailor services to meet your exact requirements.

Promotional Services

■ Need some innovative concepts to develop a new image for your company? CSP specializes in helping businesses create a unique identity in their marketplace with letterhead, corporate i.d., and support materials.

■ For brochures, flyers, and marketing pieces that capture the attention you want, let CSP create a top-notch program that's classy, cost-effective, and produces results.

■ Whatever your specific requirements, we'll work with you to develop the solutions you need. We want to be a partner in your business success.

■ ■ ■

Desktop Publishing Services

■ Does your policy and procedure manual need updating? CSP can write, edit and/or produce your internal manuals and documents.

■ For presentations and proposals that convey the image you want, let CSP handle the desktop production!

■ Conducting a special or seasonal promotion? We'll design and produce an appropriate flyer or personalized letter!

■ ■ ■

Editorial Services

■ We're professionals in all stages of copy production — from research and writing to editing and copyediting — to layout and proofreading. CSP can "word-smith" and polish all of your communications materials!

■ Need some assistance in editing materials already on hand? We can lend the professional eye you need — or create copy "from scratch!"

■ Utilizing CSP's editorial services is just like having a professional writer/editor on your staff — but only when *you* require it!

■ ■ ■

Career/Resume Services

■ We've been providing resume and career search materials for over ten years, producing more than 3,000 resumes. CSP can develop a complete resume "from concept to completion" via a confidential consultation.

■ We'll create a distinctive resume and unique cover letter that help open the doors to interviews that get job offers!

■ Use our expertise in defining your accomplishments and portraying the salient points of *your* career background!

■ ■ ■

Office Support Services

■ *The* solution to your requirements during overload periods (or when a secretary is out), for handling confidential work (performance appraisals, psychological evaluations, strategic planning documents), and providing the highest quality office services.

■ Cassette or VCR transcription? CSP can provide draft documents or final transcripts.

■ Require a professional look in the typesetting of an important sales proposal or document? Let CSP handle your special projects — or your everyday correspondence and materials!

■ Don't want to burden your staff with a large, repetitive mailing project? We can handle some or all of the aspects of a bulk mailing.

■ FAX, photocopying, overhead transparencies, database development and management, list processing, and Notary Public services are also available.

■ Think of us as a confidential member of your staff — available *whenever* you need us and *only* when you need us! No benefits to pay, no deductions to administer, no outlay for sophisticated computer/laser equipment, no costly investment in training!

■ ■ ■

Whatever Your
Requirements Are,
CSP Will Make You
Look Good!
Call Today.

to simply provide only a "laundry list" of the services you provide. Some clients may be unable to interpret from this listing how you can help them with their requirements. Include prose that connects directly to the client. For example, if you plan to provide resume services, don't just list "resume services and cover letters." Be certain to include text regarding your experience in this area (I include a line in my brochure that says I've produced more than 3,000 resumes in my years in business) as well as how you can help the job-seeking client—for instance, "Distinctive and eye-catching cover letters help to profile your unique background and accomplishments and will assist in getting the door open to the all-important interview. Let us work with you to effectively highlight your achievements and the salient points of your career experiences." Promotional copy for all aspects of the services you provide will convey the right message for your business. Take advantage of this vehicle for showcasing *your* abilities in the public relations field!

Yellow Pages Advertising

In nearly every location throughout the United States, this will be your single biggest—and best—advertising mechanism for bringing new business through the door. This is so important that I'll say it again: Your ability to get into the Yellow Pages will largely determine the likelihood for more immediate success for your business than any other marketing step you take.

At the time you arrange for your business telephone service, be certain to obtain the advertising schedule for the directory in which you'll be listed. Contact the Yellow Pages advertising department immediately to determine the possibility of making it into the next edition. Depending on timing, this could be up to twelve months away. Therefore, it's especially important to make these contacts the minute you've determined that you are going to establish a business and have arranged for a business telephone line. By the way, you can advertise in the Yellow Pages only if you use a business telephone number—you can't use your home number. This timing is so critical that as you are conducting your evaluation of whether or not beginning a secretarial services business is right for you, you may want to establish your timetable around this very important deadline.

Highly Recommended Tip
Be listed under as many categories as you can afford. Once you've determined the services you plan to offer, advertise under as many of the appropriate categories as possible—even if the listing is only a one-line company name listing with your telephone number. Suggested categories to consider (based on the services you plan to offer) are as follows:

- Copying
- Editing
- Notary Public
- Photocopying
- Resumes
- Transcription
- Typing Service

- Desktop Publishing
- Facsimile Transmission Service
- Office Services
- Proofreading
- Secretarial Service
- Typesetting
- Word Processing Service

Your own Yellow Pages may have slightly different versions of these headings or additional headings to consider—the key is to be as expansive and visible as possible. Interestingly, research has shown that while technology continues to improve the methods of keyboarding (from typing to word processing to desktop publishing), the majority of consumers and potential clients still think of "typing" when they need a document professionally prepared. And, of course, some clients actually do want something "typed" (e.g., completion of a preprinted application form on a typewriter). Therefore, it's highly recommended that you place your biggest ad under the Yellow Pages category of Typing Service (or the equivalent version in your directory), even if your competitors aren't doing this. Other than my resume service and Yellow Pages ad for that category in two different directories, my Typing Service ads have always pulled in the most new business for my company—and this has been true since I started out in 1983.

Another important factor to keep in mind is analysis of your competition (refer back to your earlier notes from Researching and Assessing the Competition, in chapter 3). Examine closely the current telephone directory: Who are your competitors? Look under all applicable categories and make a list. Where are they advertising? How large are their ads? Where are the most or biggest ads run? If your competitors have been around for any length of time, you can bet they've determined (if they're smart business managers) the categories under which it makes the most sense to advertise heavily. Take their cue and align your advertising accordingly. While you might not match competitors' advertising in the first few years, you could certainly choose to run your bigger ads in those categories where the competition does.

Another interesting thing about Yellow Pages advertising for this field is that small, in-column display ads seem to draw better than large, out-of-column display ads. Exceptions to this are usually but not always found in large metropolitan areas—New York City, for example. The single biggest factor in determining which way to go is, again, to look at what your competition is doing. If all of your competitors are running large display ads, that may be what pulls in your area. It's more likely, however, that the in-column display ad—somewhere between a half inch (most economical) and approximately 2 or 2½ inches—is the best way to proceed for this industry.

To discourage drop-in clientele (important for most home-based businesses), you can specifically request that the telephone company not include your street address in your advertisements and in your White Pages listing. You can have your post office box address included; however, there is probably little value to doing this other than soliciting junk mail. Instead, simply list your town and the telephone number, the latter in very large type.

If you opt to also advertise in the telephone directories of adjacent towns (e.g., you might be located near a major route that commuters use to travel to adjacent towns), consider including a line like "conveniently located in [your town]" as a means by which to encourage traffic. I advertise in a directory that covers three towns, two of which border my town but are currently in a different (toll) dialing area. The telephone company requires that the city name of the geography my local directory serves be included in my ad by my telephone number in this other directory's advertising. But because I want to stress my location as adjacent to these two "toll" communities, I include a line in my ad stating that I'm "conveniently located in Durham." This has attracted numerous callers from these towns who are already commuting right by my street on their way north to the next largest cities. If I didn't state that, they might think I was located half an hour farther from their homes than I am and not bother to call.

In addition to specific product offerings and new services, always advertise special features that you offer:

- Competitive rates
- Business hours, evenings, and weekends
- Notary public services
- Photocopying
- Telephone dictation
- Number of years in business (once it's significant; I always include "Serving Clients since 1983")

- Convenient appointments
- Pickup and delivery (if it's free, add that as well)
- FAX service
- Rush service
- Same-day turnaround
- Discount for referrals
- Confidential service

Try to include something "free" in your advertising, whether it's "free resume guidelines upon request," "free review of your existing resume," "free photocopies (ask for details)," or "free pickup and delivery"; these items catch the reader's eye and usually don't cost *you* that much. Obviously, something like free pickup and delivery is practical only within a certain geographic area and may make sense only for larger "corporate" clients.

Be certain to request proofs of your ads from the sales representative; push hard if this request is met with resistance. One year (early on, when I didn't request proofs) my ad was omitted from one category altogether. I received the ad free of charge for the next entire year. Another year the Yellow Pages representative showed me a sample of my ad prepared with red ink in a quarter-page size. This was to encourage me to sign up for larger ads. But the proof spelled *transcription* incorrectly and was not designed as I had envisioned it. I frequently see the word *laser* misspelled as *lazer* in a number of related Yellow Pages ads. And one of my competitors has had a misspelled word, *develoment,* in its ad for the past four years. While the initial error wasn't the competitor's—unless a proof was approved—I'm surprised a correction hasn't been requested in the subsequent years.

On the following page are pasteups of actual ads I run for my company in the Yellow Pages of two directories.

Community Telephone Directory

Some communities have their own small telephone directories, usually published by local civic organizations (Exchange Club, Rotary, etc.). Advertising in these directories is a good way to get established, a nice way to support local causes, and a viable way to begin bringing in business. A half-page ad in a small directory generally costs under $200 per year and is very visible. Design an ad yourself or use the organization's graphic design services—perhaps "blow up" your business card if you're very satisfied with what it says and how it visually attracts the eye. Consider laying out your ad in reverse (white lettering on a black-ink background).

Publicity and Promotional Advertising

Generating news and obtaining free publicity are two of the easiest and best ways to get exposure at little or no cost, particularly

COMPREHENSIVE SERVICES PLUS

Professional Editorial and Office Support Services

Laser Printing ● Word Processing ● FAX
Correspondence ● Manuscripts ● Copies
Standard & Micro Transcription ● Theses
Resumes ● Day-Eve-Weekend Appts.

Since 1983

349-0256

Typing Service

COMPREHENSIVE SERVICES PLUS

Distinctive Resumes and Cover Letters Since 1983

Consultation ● Writing/Editing
Laser ● Free Disk Storage ● Copies
FAX ● Day-Eve-Weekend Appts.

349-0256

Resume Service

COMPREHENSIVE SERVICES PLUS

Professional Office Services

Laser Printing ● Word Processing/Typing
Typesetting ● Resumes ● Manuscripts
Transcription ● Copies/FAX ● Proofing
Daytime ● Evening ● Weekend Appts.

Conveniently located in Durham

Middletown

349-0256

Typing Service
(Out-of-town directory)

COMPREHENSIVE SERVICES PLUS

DISTINCTIVE RESUMES

Consultation & Writing/Editing Services
Unique, Personalized Cover Letters
Laser Printing ● Typesetting
Free Disk Storage ● Rapid Turnaround
Copies/FAX ● Day-Eve-Weekend Appts.

Call for Free "Resume Guidelines"

Serving Clients in Connecticut & Massachusetts since 1983

Conveniently located in Durham

Middletown

349-0256

Resume Service
(Out-of-town directory)

COMPREHENSIVE SERVICES PLUS

PROFESSIONAL TYPING/ WORD PROCESSING CENTER

Serving: individuals ● professionals
large/small businesses ● students

Manuscripts ● Repetitive Letters ● Resumes
Transcription ● Photocopying ● FAX ● Notary
Weekend/evening appointments also avail.

Very competitive rates!

349-0256

Word-processing Service

COMPREHENSIVE SERVICES PLUS
Word Processing ● Laser Printing ● FAX
Standard & Micro Transcription ● Copies
Resumes ● Day-Eve-Weekend Appts.
--------------------------------------349-0256

Secretarial Service

when you are starting out. Simply starting a new business is news, and you should be certain to get the word out to all newspapers (daily and weekly) that cover your geographic area *and* the market you intend to serve.

Keep in mind that, as your business grows, you'll want to establish relationships with all media contacts in your vicinity to garner future publicity. New equipment, new service offerings, and unique promotional discounts are all potentially newsworthy items, as are celebrations of your company's anniversary. Develop a media contact list in your computer database and keep it up to date.

Yearbooks, Fund-raising Materials, and the Like

Once you're "in business," you'll quickly become the target of many telemarketing efforts—from large, national companies wanting to sell you insurance to the local Little League organization and Police Officers' Benevolent Association seeking donations. The latter groups generally want you to support their cause through purchase of an ad in a directory they are producing or in a program for a special event. It's always good to support local causes, but a word of caution: You'll probably receive more requests than you can afford, especially when you're first starting out.

Therefore, select carefully, perhaps rotating from year to year the organizations that you support. Never hesitate to say that you're a small company (one employee) just starting out, without a large advertising budget. Usually, the smallest, business-card-size ad runs anywhere from $25 in a high school yearbook to $100 in a civic program. That cost times a half-dozen different organizations can quickly add up. Ads in these types of publications do help to establish your presence and goodwill over time but generally don't directly increase your traffic or profits, at least not when you're first setting up operations. Pick and choose carefully, but save the bulk of your advertising budget for the Yellow Pages and highly select direct mail marketing. The type of direct mail mar-

Business Services Plus

MAIN STREET • ANYTOWN, USA

(343) 343–3333

MEDIA CONTACT: Jessica Turner, 343–3333

DATE: 3/6/94

FOR IMMEDIATE RELEASE

Jessica Turner of Anytown, USA, is pleased to announce the recent opening of her new secretarial service, Business Services Plus. A former executive secretary with JKL Manufacturing Corporation for six years, she has more than ten years' experience providing professional word processing and secretarial services. A graduate of Smith Business School, Your City, USA, she holds a degree in business administration.

Business Services Plus will furnish professional services to executives, sales personnel, individuals, and students in the tri-county area. From an office fully equipped with state-of-the-art computer technology, laser printing, and fax services, Turner promises to "be a partner in each client's business success." Office hours will be scheduled to suit client convenience on an appointment-only basis. During the month of April, she is offering a 20 percent-off-first-invoice discount to each new client.

Turner states, "Today's tough economic climate demands cost-efficiencies and high productivity—I can offer exactly that to each and every client." Call today to find out how Business Services Plus can service *your* company's requirements.

keting I've found most useful is mailing carefully developed materials in response to a prospective client's telephone inquiry about services provided.

Developing a Newsletter

As with a brochure, a newsletter is a perfect way to showcase your talents. It's also the ideal tool for communicating on a regular basis with your clients *and* those prospective clients with whom you'd like to do business. A recommended schedule for producing your own company's newsletter is quarterly. This is affordable yet frequent enough to maintain your image before clients. Most business operators find that once their businesses are started, attempting to publish monthly or even bimonthly is simply too aggressive a schedule to which they can adhere. Whatever schedule you adopt, it's important to be consistent and stay with it.

A beginning format that is easy to maintain is a simple $8\frac{1}{2}$-by-11-inch sheet folded into thirds. Check with your local postal authorities regarding sealing of the newsletter. Some newsletters are held together with a small circular seal. Others, such as my quarterly, are not sealed at all (per the request of my post office). Staples are almost always frowned upon.

You can have lots of fun designing your newsletter, from selecting a creative and eye-catching name for the name plate (top of the newsletter where you state the name and issue number/date) to picking out a paper for producing it. Some secretarial services use the same paper for every issue—to build on a "look" that's uniquely and consistently theirs. My method is to select a different color of the same weight and type of stock for each issue; I prefer using a recycled stock with a heavy look and feel (and include the recycled emblem on the newsletter). It almost resembles a granite finish.

You may be wondering, "What can I possibly say in my newsletter?" The key to a successful newsletter, according to experts, is providing valuable information for your readers. This can be sharing any ideas you've gleaned in the time you've been doing business for better managing time, organizing files, producing promotional copy, and the like. Also equally valuable to your clients would be articles about new services you are providing, new equipment you've obtained to make *their* life easier (or their projects look even better), new paper choices that are available—whatever. Consider including a promotional offer in some or all of your newsletters, redeemable during that quarter only (if you settle on a quarterly format). Something along the lines of a percentage off the next invoice for providing a referral, a certain number of free photocopies, or a generous discount off the consultation period for a project developing a client brochure or newsletter are good ways to "give something back" to your clients.

Never hesitate to thank your clients for *being* your clients. The quarterly schedule I've developed for my newsletter calls for mailing it during March, June, September, and December. I use the December issue for my holiday message as well as expression of appreciation for my clients choosing to do business with me. I devote probably a quarter of the editorial space available in each newsletter to "sit on the fencepost" and deliver my own editorial. Topics I've used for this personalized message over the years include the birth of my last baby, my twins' fifth birthday, and my company's tenth anniversary. I also tuck in a line about upcoming vacations, when relevant, providing advance notice to my clients of when I'll be away so that they can plan their needs accordingly.

As for the general information articles included in the newsletters, I typically write about good suggestions I've implemented for managing workload, time, and projects. Occasionally, I subtly promote various services at the same time, as when I ran an article about the benefits of developing a brochure. Here I included a time-limited offer for a free half-hour consultation; four clients redeemed this, resulting in significant billings for the development of four brochures. Two clients remarked that they were "unaware" I provided this service. You'll find, as time goes on in this business, that although you may interact with your regular clients frequently, they still may not be fully informed as to all the services you can provide to benefit their businesses. Using a well-written newsletter is a fun and timely way of staying in touch with your clients—to the benefit of you both!

CSP Quips and Clips

a publication of Comprehensive Services Plus • P.O. Box 718, Durham, CT 06422 • (203) 349-0256

SUMMER 1993   Volume 2, No. 2

Summer Daze ...

"Summertime ... and the livin' is easy."

At least, that's what Gershwin convincingly said in his heartwarming musical, *Porgy and Bess*. It's been nearly 20 (!) years since I sang those lyrics in college, but I still feel the calming nostalgia of knowing that summer, if only psychologically, offers a brief respite from the hurried pace of its sister seasons.

My excitement this season directly impacts summer office hours (we'll be closed on Fridays). I've recently signed a contract with Globe Pequot Press to write a book this summer ... although I've self-published a number of books, this is my first venture into professional publishing.

The offices of Comprehensive Services Plus will be closed for vacation from July 29 through August 6. Please be sure to check your schedule and arrange for your office/editorial requirements accordingly.

Feel free to leave messages on the answerphone; we'll return your calls promptly. *Have a sensational summer!*

Jan Melnik

Does Your Business Card Do All It Should For You?

If you're still using a 3.5- x 2-inch "standard" business card, you may want to think about updating the image this card portrays. Probably more than any other type of written material, your card *gets* your name around and *keeps* it around. Prospective clients may not retain your brochures, your letters, or your flyers ... but they nearly always save your business card for future reference. Why not consider some of the following ideas to brighten your company's image the next time your supply of business cards needs replenishing?

❖ **Two-fold.** Just adding a flap to the standard-sized card increases the printing costs only nominally on quality cards, but substantially enhances the amount of space you have to get

your message across. Whether you provide a brief summary of benefits and advantages to your customers or a listing of services offered, you'll be able to succinctly arrange this information, yet retain that all-important white space to insure a card that's uncluttered in appearance.

❖ **Multi-panel.** Adding several panels to the standard 3.5- x 2-inch card allows you to communicate even more ... and possibly will alleviate the need for carrying along additional brochures or handout materials describing your services and company at your next business conference. Plus, they can be very memorable and attention-getting. (That's the whole idea!)

❖ **"A picture's worth a thousand words."** If recognition of *you* plays a big part in your business success, consider adding your photo!

❖ Add a color — add a logo — create a slogan. Without crowding even the basic single-panel card, you can still communicate "something special" by developing a unique appearance or statement about your business. **We can help!**

Update Your Resume/C.V.

"Why do *I* need a resume or C.V.?" Maybe your resume is now five years old ... perhaps the Chamber is seeking information about you ... maybe you are preparing to expand and require an up-to-date biography as part of your loan application ... perhaps you're about to launch a new business or product line and you need to include professional information in your business plan ... it's always a good idea to have a current resume or C.V. available.

CSP can help! We've prepared more than 3,000 resumes, and we can professionally handle *your* career materials ... "from concept to completion" via a full consultation, or we can quickly update your existing resume. Through September 30, 1993, we'll give you **20% off** whichever resume package is most appropriate for your needs!

It's always a good idea to have an up-to-date resume or C.V. available ... you never know what opportunities may present themselves and require you to respond immediately!

CSP Quips and Clips© is designed, written and produced by Jan Melnik, Comprehensive Services Plus. Printed on recycled paper.

Flyers

Flyers can be developed for many purposes. From posting them at local universities and supermarkets to mailing them out as informal direct mail pieces, they can be highly effective. Once again, developing your own flyers gives you the perfect forum for showcasing your creative abilities. A simple flyer that's easy to develop is an enlargement of your business card copy or one of your Yellow Pages ads, provided that it is strongly written and has an eye-catching layout. Add a creative border or frame, use font features sparingly to create a clean look, and you're all set for printing and distribution!

Sample Flyer

Creative Business Services
P.O. BOX 333 • YOUR CITY, USA 55555

"When Your Image Counts, Call the Professionals"

We can help you with all your business requirements:

- Professionally Prepared Brochures, Newsletters, and Flyers
- Well-written Promotional Copy
- Distinctive Resumes and Customized Cover Letters
- Mass-mail Campaigns
- Transcription Services
- Editorial and Composition Services
- Fax and Photocopying Services
- Custom-designed Business Cards and Letterhead

Creative Business Services can provide whatever you need in professional word processing, typing, and secretarial services!

Call 666–2020 Today!

New and Repeat
Clientele Acknowledgments

The easiest source of new business is through repeat and referral business. Your current (or soon-to-be current clients) will provide the best form of advertising for your company—and it's free! Be sure to cultivate it by encouraging present clients on a somewhat regular basis to "feel free to take a few extra business cards to give to contacts" they might have. Always insert a business card with each completed project. You don't want to be too pushy, but if you have established clientele satisfied with the services your company provides, these individuals will frequently refer you to other, potential clients.

Be certain to follow up each project for a new client with a handwritten thank-you note. Obtain stationery for your business expressly for this purpose. I use notepaper with my business name on the $7\frac{1}{2}$-by-$5\frac{3}{4}$-inch notes (which fold in half) and my business address on the envelopes. The cost for a box of one hundred notes and matching envelopes was under $30 and well worth it for the professional look they impart. A typical message of thanks might be as follows:

> It was a pleasure working with you on your grant proposal. I'll be very interested in knowing the outcome. Thanks for giving Comprehensive Services Plus the opportunity to handle this project. I look forward to working with you in the years ahead. Sincerely,

Over the years I've had numerous clients comment on how much they appreciate receiving a handwritten note of thanks, simply for opting to do business with me. I've also noticed that my taking the time to write to my clients in turn fosters in them a desire to write back. The acknowledgment notes I've received from my clients have built an extensive "testimonial" file in my office.

Don't neglect your regular clients. It's just as important to acknowledge their ongoing relationship with your business. Because referrals—other than leads from Yellow Pages advertising—represent a significant number of new clients for my business, I want to constantly cultivate goodwill with my established client base. For those clients referring someone to me for a resume consultation, I jot a quick, personalized note of appreciation and enclose a coupon redeemable toward future services (for the *referring* client). When I consider what I spend each month with the telephone company for my Yellow Pages advertising, this is a tiny investment yielding big dividends.

Here are examples of clients for whom I've used acknowledgments:

- A landscaper, who, using the forms I created, successfully bid on a $100,000 contract (he received a thank-you note followed by a dinner out, including spouses)

- A sales manager at a major cosmetics company, who got a coveted promotion—in her case, we'd been working together for several years, and she had given me samples of products her company manufactures each Christmas, a wonderful bag of goodies (she received flowers with a balloon and, at Christmas, a gift certificate for dinner at a French restaurant)

- An insurance broker, beginning a new business and making his first sale (he received a note of congratulations)

These small courtesies cost little, yet they reap tremendous rewards in terms of continuing to maintain your image as a professional dedicated to the individual successes of each of your clients. Don't overlook, either, the opportunity to communicate with your clients when you read of news of their personal or professional accomplishments in the local papers. I always clip the article and photo and send it along with a quick little note—let's face it, when you're featured in the papers, you can never have enough copies of the article for sharing with friends and family!

While your business will ultimately gain a foothold and experience true growth through repeat clientele, you'll always need to generate a continual flow of new traffic to your office. This is essential to cultivate in order to replace accounts that "disappear" (companies that go out of business, firms that contract with you seasonally for work, companies that use your services extensively for many months but then decide to hire a permanent employee to do the same thing . . . there are many valid reasons why you will "lose" a client that have nothing to do with the quality or price of your work).

Attempt to designate a regular time each week when you work on promotional materials and advertising (including direct mail). Whether it's responding to a want ad for a part-time transcriptionist (in an attempt to sell your service as an alternative) or preparing a mailing to a group of specifically identified businesses, you'll want to devote regular, ongoing time to cultivating new business. Doing so also keeps your outlook fresh and guarantees that you'll keep "selling" those services. And always remember to update current clients on new products you are now offering. This is where your newsletter can be used effectively. Periodically (say, every six months), evaluate your client list and creatively consider ways in which your current clients might utilize some of your other services. Try to introduce clients to these other services through discount offers.

Source Tracking/New Client Inquiry Log

This can't be emphasized enough—especially in the first few years of business. It's extremely important to know the source of each and every new client: It's the only way you'll know which advertising dollars are pulling for you—and to what degree. It takes at least six months to gain solid numbers that you can analyze to determine what advertising methods are paying off for you. Always track this information from the very first point of contact, when you pick up your telephone and say, "Hello, Accu-Type Unlimited, may I help you?"

Don't get off the phone—even if it's a caller that's clearly shopping around for prices—without asking, "How did you learn about Accu-Type Unlimited?" If the caller indicates the Yellow

Pages, be sure to ask, "Under which heading?" (if you have advertised in more than one location, because it may not necessarily be obvious) and "Which directory?" (if you're listed in more than one book). Record this information on a New Client Inquiry Log (a sample follows this page) and transfer the information to a Client Work Order (see next section) as soon as you schedule the prospective caller's appointment. If business is through a referral, find out who referred this call; consider keeping track of referrals and perhaps rewarding those referring clients with an occasional thank-you—a professional thank-you note, a $5 certificate toward future services, a 10 percent-off-next-service coupon, and so on.

If you determine after six months' time that you are pulling 75 percent of your new business from one specific heading in the Yellow Pages—and it's not your biggest ad—that will give you the message to possibly enhance that ad, or at least maintain its current size, in the next year's edition. Likewise, if you get only one or two small jobs from one of the headings, you might scale back on that particular ad—perhaps running only your company name and telephone number and maybe adding the line "Please see our ad under Secretarial Services."

As time goes on and you develop experience with analyzing your advertising results, you might determine that running print media ads on a regular basis is not cost-effective—and thus reserve the newspaper ads for special giveaways, 10 percent-off coupons, and so on. You'll be the judge because *you're* in charge!

Getting back to using the New Client Inquiry Log, I try to take as many notes as possible regarding the project description and what I've quoted on the phone, because quite frequently clients will be "shopping" far in advance of when they actually need a service.

If they don't call back to schedule an appointment until a few months later, I appear very professional, with an excellent memory (which I don't have), when I pull the sheet out and reread my notes. These records should be maintained in chronological order. By the way, I suggest that you always *ask* a prospective client for an appointment.

Many first-time callers will ask my location (as I've stated previously, because I'm home-based, I never print my address in my

Sample New Client Inquiry Log

(your company name) _____

Name _____   Date _____

Town _____   Telephone _____

Project _____

_____

Deadline _____   Drop-off Date/Time _____

$ Quote _____

Why call? _____   Price shop? _____   Ck. Location? _____

Comments _____

_____   Source _____

_____   Business Close?   Yes / No

Name _____   Date _____

Town _____   Telephone _____

Project _____

_____

Deadline _____   Drop-off Date/Time _____

$ Quote _____

Why call? _____   Price shop? _____   Ck. Location? _____

Comments _____

Name _____ Date _____

Town _____ Telephone _____

Project _____

Deadline _____ Drop-off Date/Time _____

$ Quote _____

Why call? _____ Price shop? _____ Ck. Location? _____

Comments _____

_____ Source _____

_____ Business Close?   Yes / No

Name _____ Date _____

Town _____ Telephone _____

Project _____

Deadline _____ Drop-off Date/Time _____

$ Quote _____

Why call? _____ Price shop? _____ Ck. Location? _____

Comments _____

_____ Source _____

_____ Business Close?   Yes / No

ads or on my business cards and other literature). At this point I still don't reveal the specific address, indicating only that I'm off a major route in my town. Obviously, once the appointment is scheduled, clear directions are provided. For those clients who ask why the address isn't published, I tell them that all appointments are scheduled in advance and that there are no drop-ins, so as to protect the confidentiality of my clients.

This is probably all the prospective client research you can do at this point. Once you have booked a new client, however, don't overlook taking time at the conclusion of your initial appointment to state, "You mentioned you located me under Resumes in the Yellow Pages [or wherever the client saw your ad]—what made you select [your company name]?" The response will provide you with valuable information about what works in your ad, and maybe what doesn't. It might also provide information about other companies in your area, but that's not the key objective. You want to ascertain the critical decision point information in your ad that prompted this person to pick up the telephone and contact you. Moreover, you might obtain a lead about other services you advertise that piqued the person's curiosity—and will lead to your selling additional services.

It's also especially rewarding to hear from a new client something like, "Your ad looked great, and when I spoke with you, I could tell you knew what you were talking about and were very professional, so I didn't call anyone else." I always go back to the New Client Inquiry Log I maintain to add any additional information gleaned during an appointment and "close out the form" by checking whether or not the business actually closed. This log serves as the one place where I can assess on a regular basis what types of advertising are working best for me, what distinguished my company in my clients' eyes, and the types of projects I obtain from various sources.

Client Work Order/
Service Waiver/Deposit Receipt

I recommend using a multipurpose form when meeting with all first-time clients as well as with regular clients at the beginning of each major project. This is to accurately record the project description and requirements, detail directions, note the deadline, and so on, as well as to confirm client billing information, provide a cost estimate, obtain the client's signature for your records, and (with a photocopy for the client) serve as a receipt for deposits.

There is an important statement in the text portion of the Client Work Order: "Final proofreading is the responsibility of the client." This is important to you, as a secretarial service owner, because it limits your liability in the event of an error discovered after the client has accepted work.

Signage

Depending on the provisions and regulations in your own community, a small, well-designed, and generally somewhat expensive (can easily be several hundred dollars) business sign is appropriate and frequently necessary to assist in directing clients to your location. Every circumstance is unique—and whether you live in a condominium complex, apartment building, or single-family dwelling will largely govern the use of this advertising and promotion mechanism. A single-family dwelling is generally most in need of this device—either to help separate you from rows of other homes in a subdivision or to direct clients if you live in a particularly isolated or remote area of your town. Coupled with a visible and attractively placed house number, it's an ideal directional tool.

When designing your business sign (having first learned the maximum dimensions, if a sign *is* allowed), think "simplistically." You're not in the market for drop-in clientele (at least not while your business is starting out in a home-based setting); therefore,

Best Business Services

Celebrating 11 Years! • 1983–1994

P.O. Box XXX
Anywhere, USA 88888
(333) 333–4444 • Fax (333) 333–4466

CLIENT WORK ORDER • SERVICE WAIVER • DEPOSIT RECEIPT

Date/Time _____

Client Name _____

Company _____

Address _____

Office Telephone _____ Home Telephone _____

Project _____

Source _____

Font Selection _____ Stock Selection _____

Copies _____ Stapled? _____ # Originals _____ Min/Max # Pages _____

Cover Page _____

Special Instructions _____

Deadline/Pickup Date _____

Estimated Cost: _____ $ _____

Tax $ _____

Total $ _____

Less Deposit – _____

Approximate Balance Due $ _____

The above estimate is provided to the best of our ability following initial review/consultation. Final invoice is based on actual project requirements. Significant differences between estimated total and actual requirements will be discussed with the client prior to completion of the work.

A nonrefundable cash deposit of $25 is required for all word processing/desktop publishing services; a $75 deposit is required for all complete resume consultations. All written materials and consultation services must be paid for in full upon receipt of completed product; completed work will not be released until full payment is made, unless alternative billing arrangements have been made in advance. Unpaid accounts over 30 days are subject to a $5.00 monthly late charge. **Final proofreading is the responsibility of the client.**

The client hereby agrees that any inaccurate, incorrect, or misleading information in the resume or other materials provided to the client by *Best Business Services* is not our responsibility and that the client had an opportunity to review the materials and approve its entire content prior to delivery and/or reproduction. This includes the responsibility of students to insure that all components of a paper, thesis, dissertation, etc. comply with the guidelines provided by their school. The client's signature below certifies understanding and agreement with all of the statements of this document.

Signature _____ Date _____

Professional Desktop Publishing, Promotional, Editorial, and Office Support Services the sign does not need to "tell what you do." After you have selected your company's name (refer to chapter 3), you'll want to design a sign that highlights it to the best advantage. If your business name is Advantage Office Services, you might use the initials AOS on a business sign.

Other Methods of Advertising

Each community is different, but you are probably aware if there's a well-read weekly "throwaway" newspaper in your town that gets good distribution. Depending on your success in getting into your telephone directory's Yellow Pages, you might want to consider running a small ad every week in a local weekly paper to begin to build visibility and name recognition. Usually, these papers are distributed free of charge, supported by paid advertisers (you). Depending on the layout of the paper, you might choose display advertising—an attractively boxed ad of business card size—or classified advertising—ten to twenty words in an in-column classified ad under the heading of your choice. In the latter case, the heading of Typing is likely to pull the most business for a word processing/secretarial services company.

If you have a local daily newspaper, check into its advertising rates; a standby program is probably the most cost-effective way to advertise regularly. This program typically guarantees to run a specific ad once per week—the newspaper's choice of which day, and it varies from week to week—for a certain amount of time (the usual minimum insertion is four times). You usually save about 50 percent over the cost of inserting the same ad on four specific days of your choosing.

Generally, advertising in a daily newspaper does not bring the results that advertising in a weekly does, because the daily paper doesn't stay around that long. And you don't build up the image of "being in the paper every issue" (which you can usually more easily afford to do with a weekly). Also, dailies cost more to advertise in, albeit they have larger circulations. Typically, once your business advertising gets into the Yellow Pages, you can eliminate most all newspaper advertising except for occasional special promotions and offers. There are many ways to spend limited advertising dollars. Methods that are probably not as effective (or affordable) for this type of business as would be the aforementioned ideas are radio and television advertising, advertising on placemats and telephone book covers, and advertising in television guides. Low-cost advertising options you may wish to consider, especially for promoting your new business or a special offer, include inserting flyers under windshield wipers in a neighboring shopping mall (possibly employing one or two teenagers to run around placing the flyers) and placing notices on campus, grocery store, and community bulletin boards.

Not too long ago I ordered my state's relatively new vanity license plate, depicting a colorful background of Long Island Sound, for my vehicle. I had two objectives in mind: (1) to support an environmental cause to improve the cleanliness of Long Island Sound and (2) to carry some kind of message promoting my business while I'm traveling the roads. Doing this can be a challenge (in six characters or less), but I settled on JAN•CSP (figuring it will be recognized first for my name and then for the acronym of my business name, Comprehensive Services Plus). What response! I'm stopped on errands nearly every day and asked, "What's CSP?" Talk about a great opportunity for promoting the business (I never did check to determine if half of the cost of the vanity plate—for the *CSP*—was a tax-deductible expense!).

You'll find many more pinpointed suggestions for promoting and advertising your business in chapter 5 as the ideas specifically relate to building individual profit centers.

Booking Business

Converting an Inquiry to a Sale

I call this form of booking business "conversion marketing," and it applies both to cultivating new business opportunities within your existing clientele base, selling add-on or enhanced services, and to taking a first-time caller who is clearly shopping around and booking an appointment. It essentially means converting a prospect into a client. I'm sure you've probably heard, and it's true, that it's infinitely easier and by far more cost- and time-effective to increase sales within your current client base than it is to develop brand-new business. That's because you've already established a reputation with your current clients—they know the quality of your work, your responsiveness, and the ease with which they can do business with you.

So, what's a new secretarial service owner to do who has yet to build a client base? Use the strategies outlined here for closing the business with as many first-time callers as you possibly can. How is this accomplished? Let's consider the field of resume services as an example. In my own business this accounts for nearly 30 percent of my overall revenue, and it is the profit center that has experienced the most growth over the past few years (in part, fueled by the recession). In talking with owners of other services, I've found it to be their experience too that resumes and ancillary services account for that portion of the business with the highest margins—that is, the greatest profits.

The following scripts will take you step by step through the process of responding to a caller's initial queries about your resume services. I'll profile several distinct types of callers, representative of the market.

Resume Script A. To respond to individuals who don't *think* they need any service other than the basic typing of their resume.

You	ABC Office Services, hello.
Resume caller	Hi. I'd like some information about having a resume typed.
You	Great! I'd be happy to help you. All resumes are handled on the computer, with laser-printed originals provided. Do you have your resume already written and are now looking to have it professionally typeset—or do you require edi-

torial assistance in developing the content of the resume to better illustrate your accomplishments and the salient points of your career background?

Resume caller	I've written the resume completely and know exactly how I want it to appear.
You	That's fine. By the way, my name is Jane Doe—with whom am I speaking?
Resume caller	[Name].
You	Hi, [Name]. Our flat fee for a one-page resume is $XX; for a two-page format, it is $XX. You will receive one camera-ready original, as well as XX laser-printed originals on your choice of stationery.

I will just mention that ABC has been developing complete resumes and cover letters for clients for ten years, and we are specialists in presenting your background in a very professional manner. Many clients decide to avail themselves of what we call a miniconsultation, during which we would briefly review the material you've written. If you desire, we would meet for generally between fifteen minutes and half an hour, during which time I would review your resume, ask you a number of questions, and perhaps propose revisions to the actual content.

Obviously, if I believe that you've conveyed the information in a very positive light and the resume content itself looks professional and well-polished, I won't suggest any revisions just for the sake of making changes. But with my background in this field, I generally find that there are areas where I can help you strengthen your presentation to create a stronger impact and ultimately help open the door to the interviews that get the job offers.

If you decide to take advantage of our expertise, the charge for editorial/consultation services is billed at a rate of $XX per hour, so that if we meet for fifteen minutes, the fee would be $XX. Is this a service that you think you could benefit from?

(depending on response)

Now, what is your availability for the consultation appointment? We offer appointments during regular business hours as well as evenings and weekends.

Resume caller   (checks schedule, discusses date/time, etc.)

You   (give directions, confirm and reiterate date and time, and obtain caller's phone number)

Great. Do you have any additional questions?

(reply depending on caller's response)

I do require a $XX deposit at the time of the consultation. The balance is not paid until ·everything has been completed to your satisfaction at the final appointment. I do want to mention that the resume is retained in our computer system completely free of charge indefinitely—there are no annual carrying fees. Most of our clients find that they are able to update their resumes for under $XX, the minimum charge. Even if you relocate out of this area, for the price of your long-distance telephone call and a small handling charge to cover packaging of your resumes so that they travel securely, you'll find that you've made an investment and you'll never again have to have your resume 'done' from scratch.

Thank you, [Name]. I'll look forward to meeting you. One final question: How did you learn about ABC?

OPTION A (referral)

Resume caller	[Name] referred me.
You	Thank you for telling me; I'll be sure to acknowledge my appreciation with a courtesy coupon for that person, redeemable toward future services.

OPTION B (ad)

Resume caller	In the Yellow Pages.
You	In the [town] directory?
Resume caller	(yes-or-no/clarification)
You	Do you recall which category?
Resume caller	Resume Services [or wherever the person found you].
You	May I ask why you selected ABC?
Resume caller	(caller's response)
You	Well, thank you. And again, I look forward to meeting you on [date]. Good-bye.

There—that gives you an idea of how to handle callers who don't believe they need anything besides the basic typing of their resume and convert the transaction into a more lucrative sale. What does this do to the bottom line? Instead of an initial sale of between $20 and $45 (depending on the flat fee you charge for a resume), billing is as much as $75 to $100 or more. Over the years I've been in business and carefully tracked each and every caller, my records demonstrate that I "convert" more than 95 percent of all resume callers into some form of consultation and/or editorial services—enhanced service for them and greater profitability for my company.

Resume Script B. To respond to individuals who have never had a professional resume prepared and don't really know the questions to ask.

You	ABC Office Services, hello.
Resume caller	Hi. I'd like some information about getting a resume done.
You	Great! I'd be happy to help you. Let me ask just a few questions. Do you have your resume already written and are now looking to have it professionally typeset—or do you require editorial assistance in developing the content of the resume to better illustrate your accomplishments and the salient points of your career background?
Resume caller	Well . . . uh . . . actually, I don't have a resume.
You	That's no problem—we're specialists in developing resumes 'from scratch' for our clients through a face-to-face consultation. Let me tell you a little about the services we provide. By the way, my name is Jane Doe— with whom am I speaking?
Resume caller	[Name].
You	Hi, [Name]. ABC has been developing complete resumes and cover letters for clients for ten years, and we are specialists in working with clients that don't have resumes. We can present your background in a very professional manner that creates a strong impact and ultimately helps open the door to the interviews that get the job offers. We would schedule an appointment to meet face to face, usually between an hour and an hour

and a half. For that meeting you would bring any materials that you might have available; however, this is not essential. If you do have an opportunity before our meeting, it's helpful to jot down dates—month and year—and places of employment. Other than that, I will essentially pull from you all other information. After we have concluded the consultation, we'll schedule a follow-up visit. Be sure to bring along your appointment book. You would be returning to the office to review and approve the final resume—and, of course, we would make any desired revisions at that time. Upon your approval—at the same appointment—we will then laserprint XX originals of your resume on your choice of stationery. You'll also receive a camera-ready original of your resume, suitable for photocopying, if you desire.

The fee for this complete package is $XX. If you would like to have us develop a pro forma cover letter for you, the flat fee is $XX. Now, what is your availability for the consultation appointment? We offer appointments during regular business hours as well as evenings and weekends.

Resume caller	(checks schedule, discusses date/time, etc.—pickup from Script A)

Resume Script C. To respond to individuals who have an outdated resume but don't really know what they need.

You	ABC Office Services, hello.
Resume caller	Hi. I'd like some information about getting a resume done.
You	Great! I'd be happy to help you. Let me ask just a few questions. Do you have your

resume already written and are now looking to have it professionally typeset—or do you require editorial assistance in developing the content of the resume to better illustrate your accomplishments and the salient points of your career background?

Resume caller   Well . . . I have pretty much written down everything, but maybe it could use some going over by a professional.

You   Wonderful! It sounds as though you'd be an ideal candidate for what we call a miniconsultation. By the way, my name is Jane Doe—with whom am I speaking?

Resume caller   [Name].

You   Hi, [Name]. As I was mentioning, a miniconsultation is typically where we work with clients who either have an out-of-date resume and need some assistance writing about their most recent position or have written the resume but would like a professional review. We generally meet for between fifteen minutes and half an hour, during which time I will review your resume, ask you a number of questions, and perhaps propose revisions to the actual content.

Obviously, if I believe that you've conveyed the information in a very positive light and the resume content itself looks professional and well-polished, I won't suggest any revisions just for the sake of making changes. But with my background in this field, and I've been working with clients for ten years, I generally find that there are areas where I can help you strengthen your presentation to create a stronger impact and ultimately help open the door to the interviews that get the job offers. You might also opt to include a few extra minutes in our consultation to discuss tailored cover letters and the most effective way to use them.

Once we've met, I will create a resume for your approval—usually, a day or two later. You will have an opportunity to approve, revise, or edit the resume—at no additional charge. Then we go into final laserprinting of XX originals on your choice of stationery, plus one camera-ready original suitable for photocopying, if you choose.

The fee for this service is a flat $XX for the typesetting of a one-page resume ($XX if it is a two-page format), plus $XX per hour for the consultation time. You are billed only for the actual time we speak, so it might be as low as $XX for ten or fifteen minutes. If you determine that any modifications I suggest would be valuable and additional editorial time is required, that is billed at a rate of $XX per hour for the actual time spent writing. As a general guideline editorial time, if necessary, is typically half of the consultation time. So if we were to meet face to face for a half-hour, the editorial time might be fifteen minutes.

Now, what is your availability for an appointment? We offer appointments . . . [etc., picking up from Script A].

By now this is getting to be routine. But it works! Try doing a little role-playing, perhaps with a spouse or friend, to practice your skill in delivering a message that *you* feel comfortable with. The beauty of the English language is that there are infinite ways of saying nearly the same thing. If the text I use sounds stilted or uncomfortable to you, then substitute words you feel will roll out more smoothly. I've observed that callers want to be reassured that you are confident, self-assured, knowledgeable, and able to provide the right service for their requirements. How successfully you convey this subtle message will be key to your business growth.

As you will see in the next example, when you can successfully market cover letters you automatically create repeat business that, particularly in a depressed job market, can easily bring a client's billing to over the $500 mark for the typical six-month job search. Let's take a look at the script I use in my office once I've completed a resume consultation.

Cover Letter Script. To deliver to individuals for whom a resume consultation has just been completed.

You	Now that we've completed the information I need to professionally prepare your resume, may I ask how you plan to structure your job search? (*Note:* This information is frequently conveyed in the course of the consultation, so you may just launch into "Now, let's talk about cover letters.")
Resume client	Besides talking to people I know, I will be sending out my resume.
You	Have you developed a professional cover letter?

OPTION A (yes)

Resume client	Yes. I think I'm all set with it.
You	Great! Well, I'll just mention that if you decide that you'd like my editorial expertise in reviewing your letter, I'd be happy to do so. I write a great many successful cover letters for my clients. The fee is based strictly on my time, at the consultation rate of $XX per hour. Usually ten minutes is sufficient. And if you decide you'd like my assistance in typing the actual cover letters so that you're creating a cohesive resume/letter package where everything is done in the same type, printing, and stationery, I provide that service at the lower

word processing rate of $XX per hour. Typically, I can produce XX individualized cover letters and matching envelopes per hour.

OPTION B (no)

Resume client   Uh . . . a cover letter?

You   Yes. While your resume is a professional, objective statement of your accomplishments, background, and qualifications, a cover letter is essentially a marketing piece whereby you can personalize and tailor your background to the requirements of a particular reader. If you are looking primarily in one field, a well-written cover letter should ideally be applicable to most purposes—in other words, the core paragraphs could remain essentially the same on most of your letters, but the opening and closing paragraphs would be specifically tailored to each company.

I write a great many successful cover letters for my clients. The flat fee for writing a pro forma cover letter is $XX. And if you decide you'd like my assistance in typing the actual cover letters so that you're creating a cohesive resume/letter package where everything is done in the same type, printing, and stationery, I provide that service at the lower word processing rate of $XX per hour. Typically, I can produce XX individualized cover letters and matching envelopes per hour.

OPTION C (no—for budget-minded clients who are clearly not interested in personalized letters)

Resume client   No, I'm not planning on sending out any cover letters.

You   (if the client is open to suggestions) That's fine. Essentially, a cover letter can be considered a marketing piece. While your resume is a professional, objective statement of your accomplishments, background, and qualifications, a cover letter can be personalized with your background tailored to the requirements of a particular reader. If you are looking primarily in one field, a well-written cover letter should ideally be applicable to most purposes—in other words, the core paragraphs could remain essentially the same on most of your letters, but the opening and closing paragraphs would be specifically tailored to each company.

I write a great many successful cover letters for my clients. The flat fee for writing a pro forma cover letter is $XX. And if you decide you'd like my assistance in typing the actual cover letters so that you're creating a cohesive resume/letter package where everything is done in the same type, printing, and stationery, I provide that service at the lower word processing rate of $XX per hour. Typically, I can produce XX individualized cover letters and matching envelopes per hour.

Another option is to prepare a well-written cover letter but to leave it generic enough for all purposes. You would address it 'To Whom It May Concern' and not have a date or inside address. It would, however, be prepared on stationery matching your resume and is still far more effective than merely using only the 'Objective' line on your resume to define your career aspiration.

Here again, the important point to remember is constantly trying to professionally promote the services you can provide—and always with the focal point of *helping your clients*. As any successful entrepreneur will also advise, you need to blow your own horn and not be too shy or reserved in talking about what you know you do well!

Moving off the resume niche example, let's consider one of the most common reasons a caller will contact a secretarial service: the need for word processing services. You will quickly become familiar with the opening question, "Do you do just typing?" Obviously, if the client has a 171 government application form or a law school application or an application for a sales tax form, he or she really does need "typing services." But you should always use that initial contact to let callers know that in addition to professional typewriting services, you can, if they desire, provide a full range of support services: a cover letter to accompany the application, a professionally developed resume, and so on. And—this is important—if the caller is someone other than a student or job-seeker, try to quickly ascertain the nature of the person's business.

Here is a sample script.

Typing Script. To respond to individuals who call with a need for typing services.

You	ABC Office Services, hello.
Caller	Hi. I'd like some information about getting some typing done.
You	Fine! I'd be happy to help you. What kind of project do you have in mind?
Caller	Well, I've written a four-page letter that details a proposal to prospective educators about a consulting service I offer, and I need to have the letters professionally done.
You	That's exactly the kind of work we specialize in. We would be handling this on a computer with laserprinting, and we offer disk storage. Storage is provided indefinitely—at no charge to you. The cost is based on an hourly rate of $XX; a project of the size you describe would typically require XX amount of time.

Caller	That sounds reasonable. I'd like to set up an appointment to meet with you.
You	Great! I have just a few questions. By the way, I'm Jane Doe; with whom am I speaking?
Caller	[Name].
You	Thanks, [Name]. Will this letter be individualized to the recipients?
Caller	Yes.
You	We can create a mail-merge database for your use—either one-time use for this project or maintained for subsequent mailings you might wish to have us handle. If you are interested, I'd be happy to discuss the types of information you might want to have created in the database and give you an estimate for handling this project.

We can create a mail-merge database for your use—either one-time use for this project or maintained for subsequent mailings you might wish to have us handle. If you are interested, I'd be happy to discuss the types of information you might want to have created in the database and give you an estimate for handling this project.

Another point I'd like to mention is that I'm a writer and editor and would be pleased to lend my editorial expertise in reviewing your material if that's a service you'd like to avail yourself of. My hourly rate is $XX.

Finally, I do want to tell you that I provide full editorial and office support services to professionals with businesses like yours. If you decide in the future to expand your business or would require assistance in developing other promotional materials, including a brochure, newsletter, marketing piece, or flyer, we can certainly help you with these projects.

Now, looking at the calendar, would you prefer a daytime or evening appointment? [etc., picking up from Resume Script A].

Prior to the arrival of a "business" client, prepare a file folder labeled with the client's name, and enclose your business card and brochure as well as the most recent issue of your company newsletter (if you have one). If you know in advance that you will be meeting with a client who is, for example, a business consultant or a professional trainer and you have worked with similar clients in the past, have rough notes available to consult regarding your experience in this field. If I'm meeting with a client to develop a newsletter, besides my own newsletter I will have my sample file available to demonstrate possible layout ideas and styles. Following a consultation of this type, I will provide about five minutes of "free discussion," sharing any marketing or promotional tips I can spontaneously think of that may be applicable to the client's business.

The work of a professional office support services business brings us in contact with diverse professions and occupations. The knowledge we possess can become an encyclopedia to our clients, and general information (not trade secrets or confidential material, obviously) is a service we can provide as an add-on in building goodwill. Most of my current corporate clients began with initial calls—usually, rush service in nature—to get a document word-processed. By opening the door to the full menu of services my business provides, I create a wonderful path into these companies, and they make up the foundation of my regular, ongoing clientele. You will find that these are the clients that remember you over the holidays with generous gifts and on Secretaries' Day with thoughtful reminders. And they are just generally the folks with whom you can establish long and mutually beneficial relationships. I always view each first-time caller looking to get a rush business letter or document produced as potentially my next biggest client company. And more often than not, this is exactly what happens.

One of the "giveaways" I routinely present to my clients upon completion of a full brochure project—where I've developed the content, design, layout, and so forth from scratch—is a two-page synopsis of all the most creative ideas I can formulate for promoting their type of business. I find that after a brochure consultation, my head is spinning with great marketing concepts and promotional plans. I always schedule my appointments to allow fifteen

minutes of time at the conclusion of a consultation to quickly prepare this listing encapsulating all my ideas.

And you know what happens? The client is thrilled to receive
"ideas for nothing." More often than not, the client follows up
with me in developing at least some of these ideas. As I mentioned
earlier, in one of my quarterly newsletters I offered a half-hour
consultation free to every client booking development of a new
brochure during the following thirty days. In just one month I
completed four consultations for brochures. Yes, I gave away two
hours of my time "for free" through that initial half-hour of consultation to each—but my billing exceeded $2,000 (not including
printing costs), and I've got four happy clients now "hooked in"
to a new service (from their standpoint).

I never hesitate to spend a few extra minutes off the clock talking shop with my clients. I've always found that doing so spreads
tremendous goodwill—and comes back to me tenfold through
increased sales. And even if a client doesn't need some ancillary
service, chances are good that through the person's network of
contacts, he or she will refer someone who does.

Developing Increased Sales to Existing Clientele

Let your existing clients know how good you are through testi-
monials. Always save letters and notes of appreciation received
from your clients—even those quickly jotted notes at the bottom
of your invoice thanking you for a super job. I freely use these letters (with the writers' permission) in promoting ancillary services
and providing professional references.

A common occurrence is having a regular client suddenly discover, through glancing at the testimonial file, that I provide a
certain service they didn't previously realize. They'll say, "Oh, you
do that?" I quickly pull from my file not only examples of whatever
the special type of work might be but letters of appreciation from
satisfied clients. It becomes an easy sell, and it reinforces the point
that we help our clients—and ourselves—every time we remember
to mention a service that might be useful to their business.

A new profit center I actively began promoting a few years ago is an individualized program delivered one-on-one with clients on "Interview Training and Techniques." I also teach this in an adult education program in my community along with a resume workshop (excellent visibility and great source of referrals). It was a natural add-on to my resume consultation service and taps into my professional background before running CSP. I pulled the complete pilot program together in just a few hours and have sold a number of these packages to very satisfied resume clients that (1) had never heard of such a service and (2) were thrilled to know such a product was available to help them prepare for interviewing.

It's been especially useful for clients who've been with one company for a long time and haven't interviewed in ages—or for people reentering the work force after a lengthy absence. Like most of you, I'm sure, I absolutely love meeting with and talking to my clients. A product such as this allows me to spend that time in an extremely profitable way that delivers tremendous client benefits. But if I didn't promote the service, most clients would never think to ask if it were available.

Strategies for "Working the Phone"

Highly Recommended Tip

This was mentioned earlier—and is important enough to mention again: Install a high-quality answering machine as soon as your business telephone number is in operation. This is essential in order to maintain a professional office—*and* a private family life.

It is unlikely that you'll ever be available at all times, Monday through Friday, 8:00 A.M. until 5:00 P.M., when the majority of initial callers will try to reach you. Just taking into account brief breaks for lunch and coffee, trips to the restroom, and runs to the post office will mean that you are unavailable at some time each day. Therefore, it is critical that an answering machine handle these calls. Expect many hang-ups—nonetheless, the world is more accepting than ever of answering machines and the majority of first-time callers (with the exception of price-shoppers or resume clients concerned about confidentiality) will leave a message for you to return their call.

Suggested Script for Your Answering Machine

You've reached the offices of A-PLUS Office Services. We're not available to take your call just now, but if you will leave a message at the tone, we'll be happy to return your call as soon as possible. [If applicable: If you'd like to transmit a FAX, please dial 1–333–555–8888.]

Thank you for calling A-PLUS Office Services.

Please notice two things in the above script, which should be tailored to meet your needs and sound like *you*: (1) you immediately identify the company name, and (2) you give the impression, through the use of *we,* of being a larger company. This conveys an important picture, especially to corporations. When recording your message, be certain there are no background noises (washing machines, kids, television, or radio). This may require you to make the recording at midnight!

Answering Machine Features

When you are shopping for an answering machine, the following features are important:

- **Tape of unlimited length,** to take lengthy messages/dictation from clients. If you plan to offer microcassette transcription, you might consider obtaining an answering machine that utilizes microcassettes. These can then be transferred to your transcriber unit after clients use your answering machine to "phone in" their dictation.

- **Ability to set the answering feature to pick up immediately, after two rings, and after four rings.** Why? You'll want to set it to answer immediately or at the second ring when you are away from the office or on vacation; having the machine answer after four rings is the setting you'll want it on at all other times—this way, if you're at the other end of your house (e.g., if you have a baby and are putting him or her down for a nap) but know you are in a position to answer, you'll have a chance to do that before the fifth ring. And when you are out of the office delivering completed work to a client, picking up office supplies, or even going grocery shopping, you will always know that the machine is automatically set to answer after four rings without having to remember to turn on the unit each time you go out the door. When you're in your office, you can, of course, answer the phone after the first or second ring regardless of the setting.

- **Portable phone feature** as part of the answering machine. This is invaluable if you have small children and equally useful if you simply want the ability to be accessible by telephone, even if you're not physically in your office (e.g., when you're taking a much-needed break, outside retrieving the mail, or proofreading out on your deck). If, for example, you're relaxing with your children and they're playing quietly or perhaps watching a videotape and you have your portable phone with you (and your children are old enough to be safely out of eyeshot for a few minutes), you can answer a call at your discretion, walk to the doorway of the adjacent room, and still sound professional without your client picking up background "kid" noises and without having to disappear from your kids completely.

  I'm not suggesting that you be a slave to the phone; however, as a result of my own three start-up experiences (my family has relocated two times to different states since I first started my business), I recommend that, in the beginning, you try to personally answer the telephone as much as possible in order to begin to get that important first-time business. Once you have an established client, he or she will know that you are managing multiple priorities, perhaps with a family, and will freely leave messages for you to return phone calls. It's the first-time caller that, many times, will hang up and try the next listing in the Yellow Pages. You want to try to be as available as possible by telephone during business hours, Monday through Friday.

- **Hold button.** This too is an important feature because it allows you to place a caller on "hold" at any point during your telephone conversation. You would do this not only for the obvious reasons (e.g., your house telephone line is ringing, if it isn't also on an answering machine, or the UPS delivery person is at your door) but also for unexpected emergencies. A hold button is especially useful in households in which there are young children: They get into a squabble right when you're in the middle of closing a prospective new client by telephone, the baby masters climbing out of the playpen for the first time and is in fast pursuit of the family kitten, and so on. By politely asking your caller if you may place him or her on hold and then quickly pressing the button, you give yourself a minute or two to resolve whatever the situation is, while at the same time appearing professional. Think of the number of times you contact other places of business and are placed on hold. Provided that you are courteous, it's a very accepted practice. And a home business owner's saving grace!

As your business develops and you find yourself acquiring more clients and getting busier, don't feel obliged to always drop everything to answer your phone. At the point that your business has a regular flow of work and you have a two-hour stretch of uninterrupted time in which to work away on several projects having aggressive deadlines (for those with children, this might be while the kids are napping), don't always interrupt your work to answer the phone—just let the answering machine pick up. As your clientele becomes established, you'll find that you know which clients are receptive to a returned call in the evening— maybe when they are in *their* home office (again, if you have young children, it might be after the kids are bathed and in bed) and which clients can be called early in the morning (once again, if you have children and they are late-risers). This gives you a little more flexibility in managing your day—another asset to a home-based business.

Of the many electronic "gadgets" designed for the home-based business market, the answering machine with portable telephone is probably your best investment.

5

Getting Down to Business

Establishing the Physical Layout for Your Office

You're in business (or about to be)! You've hung out your shingle and purchased your equipment. You're ready to organize your office setup. Home-based businesses are operated from nearly every room in a typical house, condo, or apartment: spare bedroom, dining room, today's often unused living room, closed-in breezeway, closed-in porch, room over garage, converted garage, and finished basement room, as well as an office constructed for that specific purpose (both attached to one's actual dwelling and unattached). How to determine the best use of space? Traffic pattern is probably the single most important factor. Ideally, you don't want to escort clients into a home office situated in a spare bedroom that must be accessed through your home's bedroom wing; however, nothing precludes your doing client work on a computer located in the bedroom office but using a more centrally located dining room or living room in which to conduct client appointments. Likewise, if you have a beautiful basement office but it is accessed through your laundry room or some other area of your house that you prefer clients not use, meet with clients in an area nearest the doorway.

If you do establish an office location that is not client-accessible, you'll need to carefully manage how you conduct business. For example, it is a fairly typical practice for clients to return to your office to pick up their completed work—and proofread it "on the spot." This is especially the case with resume clientele; before having you print final originals on their choice of stationery, your clients will first want to inspect the document carefully. Consider how comfortable you will feel leaving the client in your meeting area while you run down to the basement or bedroom to make revisions while the client waits. These are considerations and, of course, point to the ideal situation of being able to work in the area in which you meet your clients. If your dining room or living room is not heavily used, you might convert one of these rooms to your office/conference area.

It is also ideal if the doorway into your office area is not the only entrance into your home. That way, if you have young children, for example, and meet with clients on Saturdays, whoever is caring for your children can still leave and enter the house without disturbing you.

No matter what space you decide on for meeting clients, it will help boost your professional image and self-esteem to furnish it as professionally as possible. Position your furniture in a manner that's comfortable for clients while they're waiting for you to finish their work. Also keep in mind that you'll want to be able to talk with clients at a table or desk area (e.g., for a resume consultation), take notes, and be able to face them (instead of sitting side by side). Rearrange furniture groupings and test various scenarios until you feel comfortable. Check and recheck lighting—both general and task lighting—to be certain you have optimum working light as well as ambient lighting that creates an attractive work space in which to meet clients. Remember that you will probably be working as much in the evening hours as you will during conventional business hours and that, therefore, night lighting must be a consideration.

Another thought with regard to office placement is proximity to the nearest bathroom. Inevitably, there will be occasions when clients ask to use the restroom. I know some people in this business that simply do not make that "option" available to their clients and direct them to a public restroom located within a few miles of their home office. I believe, however, that it is imperative to make this amenity available to clients, in spite of the slight inconvenience to you (maintaining an attractive, spotlessly clean restroom facility well-equipped with appropriate supplies is one more "janitorial" task you will have in addition to vacuuming and dusting your office daily).

It is, of course, ideal to have a lavatory or powder room located right near your office that clients can utilize. If this is not possible or if your home has only one bathroom that is for the family's use, you may want to consider decoration and storage so that a streamlined appearance is maintained (with young children's bath toys, for example, stowed out of sight). I liken the availability of a restroom at a professional secretarial service to that at the offices of any other professional—all accountants, attorneys, and medical professionals have restrooms available . . . as do hair stylists and other service providers.

Assuming you have selected your office space, consider redecorating the area to suit your personality and the image you want to convey. Select a wallpaper and color that feel good to you—you're going to be spending a great deal of time in this area, and you should enjoy entering it! Add a few fresh flowers for accent color and enjoyment when you can. Use stacking bins and file trays to neatly arrange work in progress and other papers in your desk area. If you are a naturally clutter-oriented person (as I am), try to step back from your client meeting area before each client appointment and appraise it with fresh eyes. Clear as much clutter and maintain as open an area as possible—even if you are in a tiny work space. Always keep tablets, extra pens, extra business cards, and file folders available in the area where you actually meet with clients.

If you have determined to have a work area separate from where you'll be meeting with clients and the "client meeting" area is in another portion of your home shared with the family, establish a box (or even a laundry basket) of items that can be quickly moved into this area in advance of a client appointment (and just as quickly cleared away at the conclusion of your appointment). Items to have on hand include professional publications, any handouts you may have prepared (e.g., particularly relevant articles related to interviewing skills for your resume clientele), steno pads or blank tablets, pens, copies of your brochure, business cards, empty file folders, and blank Client Work Orders. If it is convenient, you can have up-to-date newsmagazines *(Time, Newsweek, Fortune,* etc.) and/or that day's newspaper available.

A final amenity you may wish to provide to clients is a beverage. I nearly always have a pot of coffee on in my kitchen (immediately next to an office and lavatory adjoining my house) and offer a cup to clients who are (1) regulars or (2) going to be in my office for more than just a five-minute pick-up. I also make ice water available. Some service providers keep a candy bowl filled in their reception/meeting area, while others offer homemade cookies, particularly during the holiday season. While these extras aren't essential, they certainly can add to the inviting atmosphere you create for clients entering your office and working with you.

IRS Guidelines—Business Use of Your Home

Once you've determined the optimum location for your home office, you'll want to calculate the applicability of the home office deduction for income tax purposes; there are stringent guidelines with regard to exclusive and sole use. Publication #587, *Business Use of Your Home* (see the Bibliography in the Appendix), explains use tests and deduction limits to use in determining your legitimate deduction for business use of your home. Detailed instructions, formulas, and a completed sample Schedule C form ("Profit or Loss from Business") and Form 8829 ("Expenses for Business Use of Your Home") are included.

Organization

With your office location determined, renovation and/or decoration complete, and furnishings in place, you'll next want to consider organization. Let's spend a few minutes discussing some of the recommended forms and procedures you may wish to establish. Please refer to the Client Work Order form (immediately following this section as well as discussed in chapter 4). This document (or one you tailor to suit your specific business requirements) should be utilized for every single new client transaction as well as each new project for repeat clients.

Client Work Order

As the sample form indicates, the following information should be obtained:

- Date and time of initial appointment (be sure to include year)
- Client's name
- Client's company (if relevant; not necessary for resume clientele)
- Client's home (or business) address
- Client's office telephone number
- Client's home telephone number
- Brief project description (business proposal, mail-merge letters, resume, cover letters, etc.)
- Source of the business

    If from a Yellow Pages ad, include directory name and the applicable category

    Referral (include name of client or person making referral)

    Repeat client

    Other source (specify)

- Selection of font (if discussed in initial client meeting; some clients are very knowledgeable as to the exact font style and size they are seeking. If you make the selection during the actual typesetting of work, note here for easy reference).

- Selection of stock (paper) (typically used for resume work; the client generally makes the decision at the time that the proposed resume is presented for proofreading and approval. Specific color choice and name of the stationery should be noted for future reference).

- Number of copies, whether or not they should be stapled, number of originals—all as mentioned in initial appointment, if applicable; this would also be the area where number of originals and/or copies a client receives with a given project should be noted (e.g., if you determine to offer ten original laserprints of a resume with each typesetting project, you would place "10" on the "# originals" line).

- The minimum or maximum number of pages desired (sometimes relevant, particularly for student term papers where a paper must be "at least ten pages long" or "no longer than fifteen pages"; always determine from the client if he or she wants you to "play with type size" to expand or contract text to fit the requirement. I usually use Times Roman 14-point, double-spaced text for theses unless instructed otherwise *or* asked by a client to enlarge or reduce to meet a size restriction).

- Title or cover page, if not already provided by client (this would be for term papers, business proposals and presentations; frequently, clients will not remember this piece of information. This prompt reminds you to ask how they want this information to appear).

- Details related to the preparation of the project (any information not covered up to this point, including spelling of an unusual name, special style instructions, reference to a client-provided style sheet, etc.).

- Next appointment (agreed-upon date and time, whether the client will pick up the project or wants the completed project to be delivered, whether or not the client is to be called first upon completion of the project, perhaps with an actual cost quote, etc.).

- Development of a cost estimate for the project ("worksheet" area to outline applicable costs). For typesetting a one-page resume with one-quarter hour of consultation time and one-quarter hour of editorial time, the handwritten estimated cost information here on the Client Work Order form might look like this:

Typeset one-page resume	$20.00
.25 hr. consultation @ $30	7.50
.25 hr. editorial services @ $30	7.50
SUBTOTAL	$35.00

A deposit should always be collected on first-time projects with the possible exception of corporate clients (i.e., when you are handling work for a company and not an individual; I have never requested a deposit from companies for which I handle work and have had only one small problem—a company folded before paying my invoice, which was a little over $100).

Determining the amount of the deposit is a fairly flexible "science." Generally, you want to ask for enough of a deposit so that the client will have added incentive to return. While the method is not entirely foolproof, most clients will not hesitate to put at least $25 down on a resume project and $100 down (or more) on a lengthy thesis or term paper. A policy should be established for your business whereby work is not released until payment is made in full (or arrangements made in advance to your satisfaction). The same holds true for mailing work out on a client's behalf. Except for very trusted repeat clients, it is probably a good idea to request payment in advance of mailing out any completed work to a client. This is one area of business where I have been repeatedly lax—and gotten "burned" (e.g., mailing out revised resumes to clients who have relocated, "trusting" the assurance that payment would be "promptly sent" and never receiving a check). Much of what makes this business work successfully is establishment of trust and mutual respect, and to this end your own good instincts are important. As with any other business, however, it is equally vital to develop policies that are fair to *you* and your clients. (See additional information under Credit later in this chapter.)

• Determination of the approximate balance due. Note the word *approximate*. This is because no matter how precise an estimate, it *is* only an estimate. You may find on a particularly lengthy resume consultation that while you estimated editorial time to be half an hour, you actually spent one hour and developed two addendum sheets to cover all of the client's professional publications. This may not have been apparent in the initial consultation and therefore affects the final balance due. Likewise, when you are handling business proposals or annual reports, additional information may be provided midway into a project that exceeds the original specifications—e.g., a client might determine to utilize more graphic depictions of spreadsheet information you have prepared than initially planned.

You should obtain the client's signature on this form—and provide the client with a copy, circling the correct purpose at the top of the form: Client Work Order, Service Waiver, or Deposit Receipt.

Once a project has been completed, the Client Work Order should be part of the permanent paper file you maintain. For some secretarial service owners, a document of this sort is the only paperwork they maintain in a file; for my business, I prefer to keep a printout of the final original document (be it a resume, business proposal, cover letter, etc.) in my file for future reference when clients contact me for an update of their materials. The only exception to this would be a particularly lengthy document (manuscript for a novel or thesis); rather than waste the paper and devote limited filing cabinet space to such documents, these are retained only on diskette (an original disk plus backup on two additional disks). By the way, if computers are new to you and/or you haven't developed a consistent document backup process, I highly recommend backing up two separate disk copies of every document. You will probably want to keep separate disks for your large clients, but bulk together resumes on backup disks by letter of the alphabet. Resumes of clients whose last names begin with the letter *A,* for example, would all be filed on one disk.

Client Files

A secretarial services business requires filing space (at minimum a two-drawer file) to maintain not only the records of doing business but client information as well. Corrugated cardboard filing boxes provide an excellent means of archival storage. I have managed to keep my eleven-plus years of business paperwork and client files confined to a two-drawer vertical file, a four-drawer vertical file, and five cardboard filing boxes (the last stored in a dry basement closet).

What Information Should Go into a Client File

- Initial Client Work Order
- Any style sheet provided by client or prepared by operator (see next section)
- Subsequent Client Work Orders (for new projects or continuations of extensive projects)
- Original final printout of client's project (with the exception of particularly lengthy documents)
- Copy of each invoice generated for the client
- Notation as to disk onto which project has been filed (if not obvious)

Style Sheet

A style sheet will frequently be provided by clients asking you to handle preparation of their theses or lengthy term papers. Essentially, a style sheet includes spelling of unusual words or those with several correct spellings, technical terms or phrases that may be unfamiliar, special capitalization, words with and without hyphens, usage as it relates to the material being keyed, and any other preferences noted by the client.

If a style sheet is not provided, you should ask during the initial consultation if one will be forthcoming or if the client is willing to spend a few minutes with you (on the clock; this is billable time) developing at least an outline for the style sheet. A style sheet is generally handwritten and is organized in rough alphabetical order.

Duplicate Client Work Order

Best Business Services

Celebrating 11 Years! • 1983–1994

P.O. Box XXX
Anywhere, USA 88888
(333) 333–4444 • Fax (333) 333–4466

CLIENT WORK ORDER • SERVICE WAIVER • DEPOSIT RECEIPT

Date/Time _____

Client Name

Company

Address

Office Telephone   Home Telephone

Project

Source

Font Selection   Stock Selection

Copies   Stapled?   # Originals   Min/Max # Pages

Cover Page

Special Instructions

Deadline/Pickup Date _____

Estimated Cost: _____

Tax	$ _____
Total	$ _____
Less Deposit	– _____
Approximate Balance Due	$ _____

The above estimate is provided to the best of our ability following initial review/consultation. Final invoice is based on actual project requirements. Significant differences between estimated total and actual requirements will be discussed with the client prior to completion of the work.

A nonrefundable cash deposit of $25 is required for all complete resume consultations. All written materials and consultation services must be paid for in full upon receipt of completed product; completed work will not be released until full payment is made, unless alternative billing arrangements have been made in advance. Unpaid accounts over 30 days are subject to a $5.00 monthly late charge. **Final proofreading is the responsibility of the client.**

The client hereby agrees that any inaccurate, incorrect, or misleading information in the resume or other materials provided to the client by ***Best Business Services*** is not our responsibility and that the client had an opportunity to review the materials and approve its entire content prior to delivery and/or reproduction. This includes the responsibility of students to insure that all components of a paper, thesis, dissertation, etc. comply with the guidelines provided by their school. The client's signature below certifies understanding and agreement with all of the statements of this document.

Signature _____ Date _____

Professional Desktop Publishing, Promotional, Editorial, and Office Support Services

Sample Style Sheet

A–F

acetylene
cast-off (adj.)
Foucalt
beet armyworm
endopolyploidy
dog-ear (n./adj.)
carcinomatosis

M–R

nosce te ipsum
Menominee
Ripuarian
perphenazine

G–L

kickoff (n.)
gill-netter (n.)
half # sister

S–Z

thyrocalcitonin
secundum naturam
way-out (adj.)
Vinson Massif
Zephaniah

I periodically review my files to weed out any material no longer relevant. For example, as my resume clients update their resumes, I try to ensure that only the most current resume is stored in the paper files (all previous versions remain on disk, however). In addition, I maintain the notes I take during a client intake for a resume consultation for about two months; these usually number between six and ten tablet pages. After the arbitrary timeframe (and this, of course, follows the client's approval of the final resume), I will shred my original notes. This helps to keep my files streamlined but still enables me to immediately access any given client's file while I'm on the telephone, providing an immediate history of the transactions I've had in the past with this client. I find that resume clients, in particular, are always impressed by my ability to seemingly recall instantly the type of work I've done with them, down to the color and type of stationery they selected for the original printouts of their resume. This contact might be five or six years after their initial appointment. Alphabetically filed records that are handy allow for professional, timely access without having to switch disks at your computer while the client waits.

Other Relevant Forms

A Client Production Schedule (sample follows) should be utilized for each client project. You may wish to establish for each regular client a manila file folder in which you maintain this log. This serves as a good means for subtotaling work on a given project and allows for ease in invoicing. This is also a useful tool for maintaining regular client activity for those accounts to which you offer biweekly or monthly billing (discussed in greater detail in this chapter under Credit). This blank form can be photocopied onto the back of the Client Work Order and creates a permanent record of activity for a given account. When the client signs the original Client Work Order, be sure to maintain the original in your files, while providing him or her with a copy of the front of the form only.

A manila file folder should also be used at the time that you are meeting with a first-time client. At the conclusion of the initial appointment, the Client Work Order, a Client Production Schedule, and the project materials can be placed into the file folder. The folder edge should be labeled with the client's name. Next, the project should be entered onto the ongoing Project Status/Deadline Sheet (sample follows). Finally, this packet of project information should be placed in your to-do, work-in-progress bin.

You will probably find it helpful to photocopy (or have printed) a large number of the Project Status/Deadline Sheet forms and affix them to a clipboard or staple them to sturdy cardboard. As business grows you will probably update and rewrite the list at least three or four times a week, so you'll need a good supply.

This form is the "lifeblood" of your business, in terms of being the one document used to track all work in progress. Long-term projects with distant deadlines should be included, usually with an entry near the bottom of the sheet to note the overall deadline for the project as well as interim deadlines for segmented portions of it. Obviously, at the start of any given week you will eventually have an idea of your standing client projects that are ongoing in nature. But let's say that the phone rings at 9:00 A.M. on Monday and it's a new client in urgent need of a resume (opportunity to charge for rush service; discussed later). So, you schedule the appointment into the day and squeeze the return appointment into the following morning. In order to enter this onto your Project Status/Deadline Sheet, you'll probably have to bump some things down and move other things around. That business proposal you have been working on is not really going to be picked up by the client until Thursday. But you had scheduled it for completion on Tuesday, wanting to plan ahead. With an opportunity to earn extra money for a rush resume, you now shift the proposal to Wednesday.

Things progress well on Monday, you receive a few more phone calls from regular clients Monday afternoon—one with a request for one hundred copies of a form you recently designed (he needs to pick it up Tuesday morning) and one with two rush bids that need to be done by Wednesday (you schedule her for a Tuesday-afternoon meeting). As the week goes on, you've now pushed the business proposal to Wednesday evening (for final editing), just in time for that 9:00 A.M. Thursday pickup.

It's now Friday and as you look back at your Project Status/Deadline Sheet, you realize that near the bottom of the list are two notations for your own business—one to do your book-keeping for the month that just closed and one to write the draft copy of your client newsletter. Oh, well, there's always next week! Similar to saving money, wherein the experts in personal finance recommend that you "pay yourself first" out of each paycheck before paying any other bills, scheduling your own company's "work" can be challenging. It's always easy to let your own priorities slip, especially when you have a client in need—and willing to pay—on the other end of the line. This is one more advantage to being your own boss. With only yourself to answer to, *you* make the call—is it worth pushing off once again a deadline you had self-imposed? Does it create client goodwill? Does it enable you to make more money because of a rush service uplift charge? Is it opening the door to a potentially long-term relationship with a prospective client you've been cultivating? These are all good reasons to readjust your "calendar"—and write a new Project Status/Deadline Sheet. The key reasons for maintaining such a log are as follows:

1. You'll never need to worry about inadvertently forgetting to handle a client project—if you exercise absolute discipline in immediately logging each client project onto the sheet at the conclusion of each appointment (or telephone call); even if you don't write in the project in actual order until such time as you are rewriting the sheet neatly, the record is there.

2. You'll enjoy a wonderfully satisfying feeling of accomplishment as you check off completed projects over the course of the business day.

3. As your business growth warrants, you'll probably find it effective to rewrite the sheet at the close of each business day. This helps you to reassess priorities, make appropriate alterations, and plan your mindset for the following business day. When the next morning finds you at your desk, you are well-organized with a clear "plan of attack" for that day's projects and priorities—as well as equipped with a good road map for fitting in "new emergencies" and rush projects.

Client Production Schedule

Company Name _____

Client Name _____

Telephone _____

Project _____

DATE	START	FINISH	TOTAL	DATE	START	FINISH	TOTAL

Project Status/Deadline Sheet

Company Name _____

Date _____

	Client	Project	Do Work	Deadline	✔
1					
2					
3					
4					
5					
6					
7					
8					
9					
10					
11					
12					
13					

Determining Profit Centers/ Your Expertise

With the backbone of your business operation established, it's now an appropriate time to evaluate those profit centers in which you hope to be engaged while you are waiting for the telephone calls to flood your office. In reviewing your responses to the initial assessment information in chapter 2, attempt to identify product offerings that align with your expertise and experience. Some good examples follow. Keep in mind that you should probably have reviewed this information prior to arranging for any advertising, business card and brochure printing, and so on. Let's look at some of the more common profiles of typical secretarial service owners.

Secretarial/Administrative Background

If your background is primarily secretarial/administrative and you have excellent keyboarding ability and enjoy typing, manuscript and document preparation is a likely service offering for your business.

Suggested Client Types. Students (for theses and dissertations), writers/authors, and companies with lengthy proposals and manuals to be typed.

Suggested Ways of Attracting These Clients (beyond the advertising methods suggested earlier). Post notices on college campus bulletin boards (recheck frequently to replace worn and tired ads); advertise in campus telephone directories and in campus publications; seek out any local editorial clubs as well as those appearing on any of the computer user group networks; prepare direct mailings (well-written cover letter, business card, and your brochure) to large companies in your area.

Hints. Print on brightly colored (neon/fluorescent) paper. Don't mention your business name—or your name, for that matter. In appealing to university students, you'll generally have more success if you *don't* appear to be a large "professional" company (there is usually a big concern over cost, and you don't want to appear to price yourself out of the market). Yet you obviously

Sample Campus Ad

Manuscript, Term Paper, and Thesis Typing
Laser Printing/Computer Editing/Storage

Call today for a quote for your next paper or thesis. It will be professionally prepared by computer with laser printout (disk available, if desired). We provide highly competitive pricing, prompt turnaround (rush service available), and a professional document prepared to your specs.

Day • evening • weekend appointments available.
Only 10 minutes from campus!

Call 333-3333 Today!!

```
3 3 3 3 3 3 3 3 3 3 3 3 3 3 3 3 3 3 3 3 3 3 3
3 3 3 3 3 3 3 3 3 3 3 3 3 3 3 3 3 3 3 3 3 3 3
3 3 3 3 3 3 3 3 3 3 3 3 3 3 3 3 3 3 3 3 3 3 3
• • • • • • • • • • • • • • • • • • • • • • •
3 3 3 3 3 3 3 3 3 3 3 3 3 3 3 3 3 3 3 3 3 3 3
3 3 3 3 3 3 3 3 3 3 3 3 3 3 3 3 3 3 3 3 3 3 3
3 3 3 3 3 3 3 3 3 3 3 3 3 3 3 3 3 3 3 3 3 3 3
3 3 3 3 3 3 3 3 3 3 3 3 3 3 3 3 3 3 3 3 3 3 3
```

don't want to appear to be using an old clunker of a typewriter, either; stress the equipment and services you provide, don't mention cost, and make it easy for interested students to respond. Use the format with telephone numbers running along the bottom of your flyer—cut between the numbers vertically with scissors, creating an easy method for students to tear off a slip. Always print your telephone number in large type on the flyer itself so that if all tear-off slips are removed before you have an opportunity to recheck and replace your flyers, the number is still accessible.

Office Support Services Background

A strong office support/secretarial background also lends itself beautifully to providing complete office services.

Suggested Client Types. Independent businesspeople—many of whom probably operate from *their* home offices but lack the equipment, time, and/or expertise to handle their own correspondence and reports.

Suggested Ways of Attracting These Clients. Check with your local town/city hall (as well as those in neighboring communities) to obtain a list of businesses in your community (often listed in a town report in a separate tax section). Also, obtain names of companies and small-business owners from your chapter of the chamber of commerce. Develop mailing lists of identified small-business owners and regularly communicate—telephone calls introducing yourself and your service, direct mail letters with promotional offers (plus brochure and business card), promotional single-sheet flyers, and your company newsletter.

When I meet a prospective new client (or learn of a new business owner in my county), I immediately add the person's name to my newsletter mailing list and send him or her material for two years (eight issues of my newsletter, plus intermittent direct mail pieces). I recently received a project from a prospect with whom I had initially communicated more than *four years* earlier (but from whom I'd heard nothing in the interim). Because I had continued to send him my newsletter, he remembered me when his regular support person—a secretary from the company at which he'd formerly worked—was on vacation. She had prepared a proposal for a major client he was meeting with in Washington, D.C., later that week; however, there were several typographical errors (and he did not have disks available). To ensure completely matching style and font, he wanted me to redo the entire proposal—for same-day service. I was able to help him out in a critical deadline situation, and while he will no doubt continue to use his former colleague for regular, ongoing work when she returns from vacation, he's established a good backup in me. Plus, he mentioned he was thrilled to have found me and would tell others (best form of advertising there is—most cost-effective too!).

In another instance of time-delay response that underlines the importance of regular communications with your clients and *prospective* clients, many years ago I had prepared a direct mail piece (a one-page letter of introduction describing my services, plus several business cards) addressed to all the department heads (about twenty, as I recall) at a nearby university. It wasn't until nearly *two years* later that I received a telephone call from a publishing company in close proximity to the university, seeking editorial assistance. After booking the business, I asked my usual question, "How did you find CSP?" The editor I was working with had contacted the English department of the university to which I had sent my one-time mailing two years earlier, and the *secretary* who had opened the mailing was impressed enough with the content to retain my business card in her desk drawer . . . and was able to provide this editor with my name and telephone number as a possible source of editorial services. That single contact led to a very lucrative client relationship wherein I provided freelance editorial services for nearly four years. For my $5.00 expenditure in postage for that single mailing, the cost of stationery for letters and envelopes (minimal), and my business cards (I enclosed about five in each letter), I had thousands of dollars in billables to this one client referral.

Sample Letter to University Department Heads

Dear [contact name]:

I am writing this letter to introduce myself to you and the department. [In my case, I next stated, "I have recently relocated from the Boston area to Connecticut and am seeking . . . "] I am seeking freelance work as a typist/word processor, in particular, of theses.

In addition to experience typing student theses, I have extensive background in the publications field, as my attached resume attests. This includes [I detailed three editorial positions I'd held in the "professional world" prior to starting my business; substitute whatever is most relevant from *your* personal experience]. Furthermore, as the owner of a freelance word processing and proofreading service, I have handled a number of manuscripts for clients [mention any local or well-known clients for whom you have worked, provided that they have no objection to this].

I utilize [list equipment work will be handled on]. I accurately type approximately [number] words per minute, and, [if relevant] as a proofreader, I possess editorial skills. I offer quick turnaround of material, and my rates are extremely competitive. Pickup and delivery of work can be arranged.

Enclosed are several notices that can be posted for student convenience, as well as a number of my business cards. I would be pleased to answer any questions you may have and appreciate any referrals.

Sincerely,

[Enclose resume, business cards, brochure, flyer, and, optionally, professional references]

Hints. Call to obtain the actual names of the department heads for this (and any other mailing); you'll have better success sending personalized letters. All marketing experts will advise that you can greatly enhance your direct mail results if you follow up each contact by telephone within a week. I must confess, though, that this is *not* a strong suit for me (cold calling or even semiqualified cold calling), and I've never followed up my direct mail pieces with a telephone call. I'm much better making my outreaches *in writing*—and I'm very comfortable doing all the selling and closing by phone *when prospects contact me*. In spite of this, I continue to have good success with targeted direct mail. Here are some additional ideas related to reviewing the newspaper, an excellent source of business leads:

- Subscribe to and *read* all local newspapers (weeklies and dailies), scouting out any information you can glean about prospective clients.

- Search for news of someone starting a business in your area (congratulate the person and offer your services, including an introductory discount; enclose your brochure and business card; add the name to your mailing list for newsletters).

- News of someone being promoted within a company for which you'd like to work, ideally someone involved with administrative and/or office management responsibilities (congratulate the person on the promotion and offer your services, including an introductory discount; enclose your brochure and business card; add the name to mailing list for newsletters).

- Try to locate an interesting or effective advertisement (comment on how effective and well done or attention-getting a particular ad might have been and let the prospect know that you can help him or her have the same impact in printed materials with you providing assistance; include an introductory discount; enclose your brochure and business card; add the name to your mailing list for newsletters).

- Especially in the beginning months of starting a business, read all want ads for positions matching your background, interest, and experience (transcription, secretarial, office support, clerical). Develop a response letter template so that you can easily reply to every ad *quickly* (the next day is ideal). Posture the letter from the standpoint of an individual seeking freelance or subcontracted work, mentioning your company in a somewhat understated manner. Enclose a resume. I recommend against including your business card and brochure—you don't want to turn off the reader, who at this point is seeking an *employee*. You can always send a second mailing of your brochure and business card at a later point.

Sample Letter in Response to Advertisement for Employment

Dear [contact name]:

This letter is in response to your recent newspaper advertisement for a [position title].

As my attached resume attests, I have professional editorial experience and am a very skilled word processor, editor, and proofreader. I am seeking to provide word processing/freelance editorial services through my home-based business, ABC Typing Services. I have extensive experience handling manuscripts; my resume details some of the background I have acquired at the publishing companies of [etc.]. In addition, I have handled a number of manuscripts for clients [mention any local or well-known clients for whom you have worked, provided that they have no objection to this].

I utilize [list equipment work will be handled on]. I accurately type approximately [number] words per minute and, [if relevant] as a proofreader, I possess excellent editorial skills. I am also an experienced transcriptionist.

I can offer quick turnaround of material, including pickup and delivery services, as well as handle "rush" assignments. My compensation requirement is negotiable and very competitive, considering the quality of my work, my background and experience, and the computer/word processing equipment that I own. If you employed me as a subcontractor/freelancer, you would not need to add to your payroll, provide costly fringe benefits, or handle social security/withholding deductions.

If you would like to explore a possible working arrangement, I'd be pleased to meet with you and discuss this further, in particular, if you are not successful in finding qualified administrative candidates to work in-house. At that time I would be happy to present a portfolio of my work. I am a very motivated and hard-working professional and believe that I would be an asset to your organization. I can be contacted at 777–7777. Thank you for your consideration.

Sincerely,

[Enclose resume and professional references]

In attracting clients through advertising, some of your responses will be immediate and clearly linked (e.g., a prospective client telephoning you and arranging for your services as a result of seeing your ad in the Yellow Pages when the person was searching for an appropriate business to handle his or her needs). Many of your clients will contact you as the result of referrals by other satisfied clients. But a sizable percentage of business will ultimately come your way that may not necessarily be aligned to any single thing you did. This also emphasizes the importance of really querying first-time clients to find out some of the underlying reasons for their contact. Do this at the conclusion of your first transaction when they have reviewed the completed project you handled, have expressed satisfaction, and have paid you.

For example, we've already discussed pursuing further those clients that say they located your business in the Yellow Pages ("Which directory?" "What category?"). It's also important to understand *why* they selected *your* company. Unless you're the only company listed under the category they consulted, try to find out why they made the choice they did. Sometimes it's location ("You were the only company in my hometown" or "You're located near where I work"). Often, however, you'll be provided with valuable feedback:

- "You were the only one who actually answered the phone, and I didn't want to leave a message on an answering machine" (frequent with resume callers who might have concern over confidentiality).

- "Your ad looked professional and listed the services I was looking for" (it can really pay off to spend a little more on your ad to detail specific *benefits* to your prospective clients).

- "The free offer attracted me" (free copies, free resume guidelines, free pickup and delivery, free ten-minute review of resume, etc.).

- "The fact that you offered appointments at times other than strictly 9:00 to 5:00."

- "I called a lot of places, but you really sounded interested, professional, and able to help me."

- "Your prices sounded fair" ("the best," "the lowest," etc.) or "Even though your prices *weren't* the lowest, you sounded like the person best able to help me."

Great stuff! And very valuable marketing information to have—and utilize—in growing your business. Never overlook too the spin-off effects of some of the other types of advertising you do. While a recent flyer with a promotional offer you send to prospective clients may be what spurs them to respond and book an appointment, the fact that you have regularly run an ad in the weekly tabloid newspaper, have an ad or two in the Yellow Pages, and have recently been featured in a local newspaper story have all helped to assure this client that you are a viable business with "staying power." Occasionally, in spite of the grilling I professionally and quickly do with my new clients, some will neglect to mention until later, sometimes many months later, that they noticed a story about me in the newspaper or also checked under different headings in the Yellow Pages before contacting me, noting that because I advertised in so many places, I really appeared to "know my stuff."

I liken this type of advertising response to the manner in which many of us view new businesses—for example, the new restaurant in town. See if some of these points don't apply to your actions too:

- Before you consider going to a new restaurant, you ask around to see if others have tried it—and liked it.

- You watch the newspaper for an ad to appear, or a special discount or offer (the popular "two-fers")—or you look for a direct mail piece with an offer to appear in your own mail.
- You watch the newspapers for early reviews and publicity articles.
- You want to make sure the restaurant stays in business, irons out the bugs, and so on, before trying it.
- You are too busy to get around to visiting the restaurant until many months go by.

Well, all of these points can apply to the way in which your community (all potential client prospects) may first react to your business—they hopefully read the press release about your start-up business in the local newspaper; they see a flyer under their windshield or at the local supermarket; they think, "Yeah, it might be a good idea to have my resume updated"; they read another story about you in a different local newspaper; they see your ad regularly in the papers; they recall that they'd initially thought about finding that old resume and getting it "polished up"; they receive a direct mail piece about a special offer you're running; they lose the ad but remember you're right in town, so they look in the Yellow Pages and there you are: They call and book the appointment. Which form of advertising actually caused the client to contact your business? *All of them!*

Now that we've explored profit center possibilities for those with a heavy typing/secretarial background, let's move on to the next area of potential service offering.

Transcription and/or Medical Background

If you have Dictaphone experience and enjoy transcription and/or have a medical background, this can be an excellent profit center—or be your sole business, if you desire.

Suggested Client Types. Doctors and psychologists (for medical reports, psychological and custody evaluations, etc.); companies (who wish transcripts made of VCR tapes: transfer to audiocassette tapes first); and town and city commissions (to provide transcripts of meetings and hearings).

Suggested Ways of Attracting These Clients. Most of these prospective clients will find *you*—usually in the Yellow Pages. But, by closely watching the employment classifieds *on a regular basis*, you can ensure immediate responses to those companies and practices seeking help. Use an introductory cover letter (as shown in the earlier sample).

Recording Secretarial Background

If your secretarial background includes experience with providing meeting minutes, this is a very profitable business to offer (*if* you enjoy providing this type of service and *if* you enjoy having "evenings out" on a fairly regular basis; for those with young children, you must be able to arrange for child care in your home evenings while you attend meetings—e.g., "Dad's time with the kids"). Plus, if this is a service area you think you'd like, you'll probably find that you will especially enjoy the chance to leave your home office on a regular basis—while getting paid and "being professional." For any home-based business owner, it's imperative to "get your nose out of your office" on a frequent basis and talk with other people. Isolation is important to guard against.

Suggested Client Types. Condominium associations (for meeting minutes; usually requires attending a meeting one evening per month to take minutes and then providing typewritten minutes within a week); town and city commissions (again, for meeting minutes; many of these groups meet twice monthly); board of education meetings; and company annual meetings (this, however, would require your availability during daytime business hours, which means time away from developing your own business, answering the telephone directly, etc.—there are always trade-offs in any business!).

Suggested Ways of Attracting These Clients. Contact property management companies and/or realtors in your area for a listing of contacts at local condominium associations. Check with your own town as well as neighboring towns; the town/city clerk's office is probably the best source of leads for opportunities with any local commissions or boards. Check with the central offices of any school districts in which you might have an interest to determine schedules of meetings for the boards of education. Think of every "job" you accept in this area as a method of networking. You will probably find that the hourly rates offered are not comparable with your own rates and are perhaps even laughable. If you become affiliated with a medical/psychological practice, for example, handling the work of a group of professionals, your opportunity for networking is multiplied. Likewise, if you become a recording secretary for a professional group or commission in or near your community, each member of that group represents a networking opportunity *and* is a potential client. In addition to all of these "future prospect possibilities," you greatly enhance your visibility within any community for which you provide support to a community-based commission or board. Your mailing list of prospective clients increases and will inevitably produce business for other aspects of your service that are likely to be more profitable than simply generating minutes.

I have provided minutes preparation services (attending meetings, then generating minutes) for a number of years for two condominium associations and my town's Board of Education and Planning and Zoning Commission. For the condominiums I set rates that are commensurate with my hourly fees for creative/editorial services but are substantially discounted because of the informal continuity of service contract. For any governmental or school work, however, you can expect to be offered significantly less than your typical hourly fees (in most cities and towns, budgets are set that provide a specified rate for services of this type, and, unfortunately, the value is significantly underestimated, in my opinion). Nonetheless, I personally love participating in activities within the community and being informed as to what is going on in my own town, and I enjoy the visibility. In addition, these relationships have cultivated many spin-off assignments—from project management assignments to complete resume package development for a number of members, to interesting transcription work (memoirs), to complete newsletter and brochure development. All of these adjunct services are booked individually by various commission and board members and are priced using my regular fee schedule.

Legal Secretarial Background

If you have a legal secretarial background, seek out attorneys and planning agencies for their overflow work. Also consider becoming a notary public and offering this as an adjunct service (useful regardless of your specialty). Advertise notary services as "no charge." This builds goodwill and opens the door to other business. It's easy to pass the simple examination. The fee varies from state to state but is usually $40–$100 for a four-year term. The cost of a stamp and seal is generally an incremental $30 or so. You can obtain information from your local governmental office (town or city clerk) or your secretary of state's office.

Suggested Client Types. Attorneys, legal assistants, and governmental agencies form the likely candidate pool.

Suggested Ways of Attracting These Clients. Direct mail pieces, with regularly planned follow-up correspondence (your company newsletter is perfect) to a prospective client database you develop after consulting the Yellow Pages, are ideal.

Human Resources/Editorial Background

If you have strong interpersonal and editorial skills, and particularly if your background includes human resources/interviewing experience, a resume service is a very lucrative and challenging business for which there is an especially great demand. A listing in your Yellow Pages is a prerequisite here because, besides referrals, that will be primarily your sole source of new business in this area.

Suggested Client Types. From about-to-graduate students to white-, blue-, and gray-collar professionals and workers, to teachers, physicians, business owners, and day care providers, nearly every person from age eighteen to eighty is a potential candidate for a professionally developed resume or CV. Even people who are not in the job market benefit from having a well-prepared resume (those starting up a business will need one for their business plan; civic leaders and those who volunteer in the community will need one, particularly if they are seeking elected office on a local commission or committee; company owners and individual contributors who wish to be public speakers will need one—the list goes on and on).

Suggested Ways of Attracting These Clients. Beyond your all-important Yellow Pages advertising, be certain to encourage referrals through coupon offers to your current resume clients. Include a "dollars-off" coupon in the folder of their completed work, offering them a future discount for every referral that turns into closed business for you.

If you possess expertise and interest in this area, plus are a skilled public speaker, offer to give a lecture or miniworkshop on writing and updating resumes and cover letters in your community. Adult education programs, public libraries, and the like are always looking for good speakers on this timely topic. (I've picked up some nice visibility, while earning a stipend, by teaching in an adult ed program.) You typically will earn a small fee through adult ed programs, plus enough to cover any expenses incurred (e.g., for copying costs of handout materials). Most libraries will offer you publicity in exchange for the time you provide at no charge. These are great ways to gain visibility for your expertise and service in these areas. Be certain to include a description of your services in any handouts you prepare, and offer a discount to any participant in these programs who books a consultation with you.

Basic requirements for success in the resume service business include your ease in meeting with many clients of diverse backgrounds and your ability to *quickly* ascertain salient points through face-to-face consultations and then concisely and relatively quickly assemble a well-written resume that is distinctive, professional, and attractively formatted.

Also important is the ability to offer appointments to meet the needs of clients who may be unavailable during business hours. If you can offer one or two evenings of appointments each week, plus perhaps Saturday mornings, this is a *big* competitive plus— and is something you should mention in your advertising. Not so incidentally, this happens to be a perfect profit center to specialize in at the onset of your business start-up if you are planning to continue a position on a part- or full-time basis during daytime business hours while grooming your own business at night. If offering evening and weekend appointments is not compatible with your own personal or family goals, however, you might opt not to enter this field. Most clients of this service will expect you to be available on a fairly regular basis at other than traditional business hours. If you do make a commitment to this profit center and hone your interviewing and writing skills, you'll find it's probably the single most profitable word processing type of service there is, with built-in residual business, since after having a resume prepared, most everyone needs professional cover letters, follow-up letters, and, ultimately, updates to their resume.

I have offered resume services from day one, and at last count I have written and/or typeset more than 3,200 resumes. And while I haven't counted, I've written probably twice that many unique cover letters. I particularly enjoy this aspect of a secretarial services business because of the diversity of clients I meet, the rewarding feeling of providing a highly valuable service to clients very much in need, and the bottom-line profitability of this profit center.

Refer to the scripts related to promoting and selling resume services included in the Booking Business section of chapter 4. The following information details the techniques I've developed and use to conduct successful resume consultations. This is intended to provide a brief overview of the manner in which a resume consultation can be conducted by a secretarial service operator with expertise and interest in this field. It is by no means comprehensive or all-inclusive; the years of background and experience I've had in this field could fill another volume. In addition, sample resumes will not be included, because there are literally thousands of professional formats and styles that can be used. Specific examples will be shown, and I'll try to share the key areas to cover for those secretarial service owners possessing the experience to appropriately deliver this profitable service offering.

Conducting a Successful Resume Consultation

- Have resume materials assembled in the area where the consultation will be conducted—blank tablets,* several pens, Client Work Order (partially filled in with information gleaned when the appointment was scheduled), appointment book (for scheduling a return visit to approve the resume proof), and any articles or handouts you may have prepared for resume clients (always give full credit to the writer or publisher of each article and also include a line like "Provided courtesy of Busy Secretarial Services").

- I conduct client consultations at a conference table (sitting, again, at right angles to each other). I also have a large wraparound sofa in my office, but I've attempted conducting consultations using the sofa and find it's not as easy for me to take notes and doesn't

---

* Besides handwriting your notes, there are two other options for conducting a resume consultation. Some service providers will tape-record the entire consultation and either transcribe or listen to the tape later, when actually writing the resume. I recommend against this practice, for two reasons: First, you will expend at least as much time as, if not more than, you did in the initial consultation getting to the same point you could have had you taken concise handwritten notes in the beginning. This will greatly reduce your efficiency (and profitability). Second, I believe most clients will respond more confidently, naturally, and comfortably if you do *not* tape-record their responses. You'll elicit better material to use in writing the resume.

The other option you may wish to experiment with is doing the consultation intake at your computer (either desktop or notebook). I have tried both methods. Before purchasing my Mac Powerbook, I would bring one of my client chairs right beside mine at my large desktop computer and type in responses while the client talked. *I* wasn't comfortable with this, because the client could see everything I was typing in—a lot of what a client will discuss, while important to my overall understanding of a client's background, is superfluous when it comes to writing the resume—yet if the client saw me *not* typing in something, he or she sometimes became uncomfortable or possibly intimidated ("Why isn't that considered important? It must not be . . .").

When I purchased a Powerbook, I could at least position it at an angle when working with a client at my conference table (I never sit immediately opposite a client; instead, we sit at right angles to each other). I found, however, that the Powerbook still created a barrier I was not comfortable with and simply found it more user-friendly to take notes on paper (a mix of shorthand and abbreviated English). At the time of writing the resume, I did not find it quickened the process any to have five or six partial pages of double-spaced notes already in the system; I start with a blank page to create each new resume anyway. Certainly try various options to determine which method you like best!

feel as comfortable/professional. Once again, you have to find the location that's most workable and natural for you and your clients.

- When a client arrives, I offer coffee or ice water before we get started. Once settled, I pull out the Client Work Order and review proper spelling of the client's name; use of a middle initial, *Jr., III,* or any other designation; address (permanent and school, for students); and telephone number (most clients wish to list only their home telephone number).

- Then I launch into easily paced questions designed to elicit the relevant information I need to write the resume while at the same time allowing the client to become confident and comfortable in responding. I have not used a questionnaire for the past nine years, but I did use a simple form when I first started. A sample questionnaire follows this section and includes basic information you may want to use if you feel most comfortable starting out with this. I recommend against asking clients to fill out the questionnaire; instead, use it as a tool to guide your questions and to ensure not overlooking any key areas.

- The main components of what is the most popular form of a resume (chronological) are name/address section, objective (optional), summary of qualifications (also called skills summary, key accomplishments, or, simply, summary [optional]), professional experience, internships, licensure, educational background, military background, professional interests, special skills, recognition/awards, civic/community organizations, publications, speaking engagements, and mention of professional references (always an addendum, if used). Not all of these components will be on every resume, of course.

  NOT INCLUDED ON A RESUME: Any personal information—marital status, number and/or ages of children (except possibly for a woman reentering the job market after a long absence raising a family), religious denomination, personal hobbies and interests (unless possibly indicative of perseverance, determination and drive, as with a marathon competitor), height, weight, age, birthdate, social security number, or salary (current or anticipated).

- The first area of questioning centers on the purpose for developing the resume. This is important because it's not always obvious. This knowledge allows for asking relevant questions and delving in appropriate depth into those areas of the client's background most related to the purpose of developing this resume.

Sometimes a client will be updating the resume for internal use within his or her own company, possibly for promotion purposes. This type of resume has an entirely different slant and level of detail than one used externally from the company.

Occasionally, a resume or CV will be developed for professional purposes, ranging in use from speaking engagements to membership in a professional association and from providing biographical information for a publication to submitting the resume to an alumni magazine.

Clients will periodically want to have a resume written simply to have a professional documentation of their accomplishments and career background without any other planned purpose *at this time* (somewhat rare, as most resume clients need their resume "yesterday" to respond to an immediate opportunity).

Clients will also seek preparation of a resume to accompany a business plan, a law school application, or a myriad of other professional interests.

Finally, the majority of resume clients *will* be obtaining a resume in order to pursue employment for any one of the following reasons: They may be seeking a change in company, profession, or field; they may or may not be currently employed; they may be a new graduate and never employed in their intended field; they may be newly discharged from one of the armed services; they may be newly laid-off or newly released from an incarceration facility; they may have opted for a "golden handshake" agreement with a large corporation that's undergoing "right-sizing"; or they may be returning to the work force after a lengthy absence (child-rearing typically being the most common reason for this).

- The order in which I prefer to ask questions, after establishing the purpose for writing the resume, is professional experience first (beginning with the most current or recent employment and working backward), then education. For new graduates we discuss educational background first, then employment.

Under the category of professional experience, I ask the name of each company and the town/state in which the firm was located (do not include street address, zip code, or telephone number; *do* advise clients to maintain this information in their permanent files somewhere, though, because it is frequently requested on job applications). I obtain the title of each position held and the timeframe for each position. Depending on the individual's overall background, sometimes just the year is adequate (1988–Present); in other instances it's necessary to provide the month and year (either a format such as Apr. 1988–Mar. 1992 or 4/88–3/92, depending on the overall layout of the resume).

If the client has held more than one position with any company, the total period of employment with the company is noted next to the company name (formats vary), with the actual timing of each position noted in parentheses after each title. Example:

1980–Present   ABCD Corporation • Anytown, USA
                Chief Financial Officer (1990–Present, Promotion)
                [description of accomplishments, key responsibilities—
                eight to twelve lines or so]

                Controller (1986–90, Promotion)
                [description of accomplishments, key responsibilities—
                six to ten lines or so]

                Staff Accountant (1980–86)
                [description of accomplishments, key responsibilities—
                no more than four to eight lines)

As the timeline goes backward, increasingly *less* space should be devoted to each position.

For students it is most likely that their "professional background" is really not (i.e., professional), and this section should be captioned "employment experience" or just "experience." For students and those clients possessing master's or doctorate degrees, educational background should be listed *before* professional background or employment experience. For most all other clients, professional experience would precede educational background.

Concerning education, mention the most recent/advanced degree first, followed in decreasing order by other degrees held. As the person preparing the resume, you are not responsible for verifying the authenticity of any information provided by the client (hence the reason for a service waiver block on the Client Work Order form). If, however, the client asks your professional advice, I recommend responding that it is of utmost importance to be absolutely honest and accurate in providing information for the resume. Education is an area that will frequently come up in discussion with clients, typically those without any formal education beyond high school. It is perfectly fine to list a college attended (provided a degree is not mentioned) *or* to mention "pursuing studies toward a degree in business administration" (again, if this were in fact true). Occasionally, I will work with clients who have completed extensive training through various corporate workshops and the like—this is certainly appropriate for inclusion (if very lengthy, as an addendum to the resume). Generally, class standing and GPA (grade point average) are not included unless the resume is for a recent graduate or the ranking/number is significant. Mention of honors status (cum laude, magna cum laude, or summa cum laude graduate) should be included, as would status as the class valedictorian or salutatorian.

High school is mentioned only in the case of recent college graduates who have minimal work or internship experience. This information is dropped as soon as there is valid professional information to replace it.

For recent graduates extracurricular activities/athletics (collegiate and possibly high school) are listed. The list does not need to be all-inclusive, depending on space available; however, it should be representative as to breadth of interest and reflect election to any positions of leadership.

- Military experience should be mentioned briefly, unless you are working with someone with a full military career; if so, then expand this background, handling it exactly like professional experience.

- The breadth and depth of community and civic background varies extensively among clients. Typically, mention is made of any organizations to which a client has belonged or does belong. Also included would be any elected positions held and the years of membership in an organization. For individuals possessing extensive civic experience and minimal professional experience, accomplishments and highlights can be expanded in this section of the resume.

- Licensure, be it licensing in health care, special equipment operation, or real estate, would be briefly mentioned in one or two lines in this section.

- Professional association memberships are also listed, with usually one line devoted per entry, along with mention of election to any positions of leadership.

- Briefly mention any relevant awards, recognition, and honors received in this section of the resume.

- Special skills can include computer skills (particularly hardware/software familiarity and expertise), additional training in a particular field, foreign language fluency (written and oral), extraordinary typing speed, and so on.

- With regard to references *if* space allows, it is permissible to state at the very end of a resume "Professional references provided upon request" *or* "Excellent references available upon request." This is optional and space-dependent. I always provide a typed version of a client's references at no charge when they have been presented to me at the time of a full resume consultation. I match the format established for the name and address/telephone information at the top of the resume, repeating it at the top of the reference page, then list no fewer than three and generally no more than seven references (with no more than two "character" references). The name of each person is listed, followed by professional title, place of employment, address (home or office), and telephone number (indicating whether it is home or office). Clients should be advised that the reference sheet is typically not mailed directly with the resume, unless so requested. It is usually provided during the course of an interview.

• Discussion of the inclusion of an objective statement (which, if used, appears immediately beneath the client's name and address/telephone number) and a summary of qualifications is intentionally left until last. Once a full resume consultation is nearly complete, I'm in a good position to assess a client's strengths and accomplishments and can determine if the use of an objective statement and/or a summary of qualifications would be beneficial for a particular client; at that time, I make the appropriate recommendation. This may not necessarily be the case, and if inappropriate, I, of course, do not mention it. Generally, an objective statement is used only for clients opting not to use customized, individual cover letters in a conventional job search. I usually advise against generic objective statements as they are typically so watered down as to be nothing more than a waste of valuable space. ("A challenging position utilizing my background and experience that will provide opportunity for growth based on demonstrated performance," etc. are all too commonly used.)

A caveat, however—and this relates to all aspects of being in the secretarial services business—*the customer is always right.* I will occasionally work with a client who wants things a certain way—if he or she is amenable, I will discuss professional recommendations. But I always allow the client to make the final decision, and this doesn't always match my suggestion. That's what this business is all about. More often than not, though, clients appreciate your professional opinion. Particularly in the area of career development and resumes, if you are an expert in the field, your recommendations will be appreciated.

With regard to the length of a resume, as a *general* rule (and there are too many variables to list here), resumes should never exceed two pages. For new college graduates and those with less than five to eight years of professional experience, a resume should not exceed one page. Although for anyone a one-page resume is *preferred*, an exception exists when a client's professional background numbers fifteen or more years, is with three or more firms, and/or reflects extensive community/civic or military experience, coupled with solid accomplishments and qualifications. A two-page format is perfectly appropriate in such cases. For clients with extensive professional speaking experience and/or publications to their credit, this information can be developed on pages that form an addendum to the resume.

At the conclusion of a resume consultation (for a full consultation, this can be anywhere from forty-five minutes for a new college graduate to about two hours for an experienced professional with a significant background spanning a number of years), clients should be asked if there is any additional information they would care to provide. The follow-up appointment should then be scheduled and the client informed that at the time of the follow-up appointment, a draft of the resume, which will resemble the final product, will be presented. The client should also be made aware that any changes and revisions to the resume will be made during the follow-up appointment, and final printing of original resumes will be handled then as well. A deposit should be collected at the conclusion of the consultation, and the client should be advised of the approximate balance due (or an exact amount, if the client contracted for a package price). Finally, thank the client for the opportunity to work with him or her and encourage the person to feel free to contact you over the next day or two if he or she recalls any other relevant information that should be included.

Resume Questionnaire

Date _____

Client Name _____

Address _____

City _____ State _____ Zip Code _____

Telephone Number to Use on Resume _____

Professional Experience

Place of Employment _____

Town/State _____

TOTAL Time with This Company (in Months/Years) _____

Title of Most Recent/Current Position _____

Timeframe in This Position _____

Key Responsibilities/Accomplishments _____

_____

_____

_____

_____

_____

_____

_____

_____

_____

[Areas to address: number of direct/indirect reports; human resources responsibilities (recruiting? interviewing? hiring? training? supervising? managing?
developing? terminating? assessing of performance? preparing/administering
salary plans?); any programs developed/implemented; for sales professionals—performance to quota and time period, results, increase by X
percentage, any cost savings or productivity gains (in $'s/%'s), etc.]

Place of Employment _____

Town/State _____

TOTAL Time with This Company (in Months/Years) _____

Title of Position _____

Timeframe in This Position _____

Key Responsibilities / Accomplishments _____

_____

_____

_____

_____

_____

_____

Place of Employment _____

Town/State _____

TOTAL Time with This Company (in Months/Years) _____

Title of Position _____

Timeframe in This Position _____

Key Responsibilities / Accomplishments _____

_____

_____

_____

_____

_____

_____

[Copy above 8–10 times.]

Education

[for recent graduate, G.P.A. (if above 3.0) or ranking in class (if in the top 25% or better)]

College/University _____

Town/State _____

Degree Held _____ Year Earned _____

Major _____ Minor _____

College/University _____

Town/State _____

Degree Held _____ Year Earned _____

Major _____ Minor _____

College/University _____

Town/State _____

Degree Held _____ Year Earned _____

Major _____ Minor _____

Licenses Held

Type _____ Year _____

Type _____ Year _____

Type _____ Year _____

Type _____ Year _____

Type _____ Year _____

Internships

Institution/Company _____

Town/State _____

Position Title _____ Months/Years _____

Highlights _____

Institution/Company _____

Town/State _____

Position Title _____ Months/Years _____

Highlights _____

Institution/Company _____

Town/State _____

Position Title _____ Months/Years _____

Highlights _____

Institution/Company _____

Town/State _____

Position Title _____ Months/Years _____

Highlights _____

Military Background

Branch of Service _____

Locations (if Relevant) _____

Position/Rank Achieved _____

Years of Service _____

Honorable Discharge? _____

Key Accomplishments /Special Recognition / Awards_____

_____

_____

_____

_____

_____

Special Skills

Computer? Hardware/Software _____

_____

_____

_____

Language? Fluency—Verbal/Written _____

_____

_____

Civic/Community Memberships

Organization Name: Years Involved: Positions Held:

_____

_____

_____

_____

_____

_____

_____

Professional Memberships

Organization Name: Years Involved: Positions Held:

_____

_____

_____

_____

_____

_____

_____

Recognition/Awards

_____

_____

_____

_____

Publications

Article Title: Name of Publication Appearing In: Coauthor?   Year:

_____

_____

_____

_____

Speaking Engagements

Topic/Speech Title: Name of   Keynote   Year:
                  Organization Addressed: Speaker?

_____

_____

_____

_____

Ideas around Objective Statement (if Used)
(Professional/Career Goals)

_____

_____

_____

_____

_____

Ideas around Summary of Qualifications (if Used)
(Characteristics, Traits, Attributes, Key Accomplishments)

_____

_____

_____

_____

References

Name _____

Title _____

Company_____

Address _____

City/State/Zip Code _____

Home Telephone _____ Office Telephone _____

Name _____

Title _____

Company_____

Address _____

City/State/Zip Code _____

Home Telephone _____ Office Telephone _____

[Copy above 8–10 times.]

[*Note:* Even if you are using a questionnaire form, you should always have a blank tablet available for recording additional information at the time of the consultation.]

Product Mix

Unlimited combinations of product offerings can constitute the successful desktop publishing, word processing, and/or secretarial service. Initially, you'll probably find yourself saying yes to nearly every request in order to begin to build your business. As time evolves, you may find that you enjoy certain areas of the business more than others or that specific products and service offerings are more profitable than others. These "revelations" will help you to determine the future direction of your business.

Some secretarial services specialize in only one or two service offerings and find that these are quite profitable and that they are satisfied with their business growth. I consider myself a generalist with expertise in a lot of different areas; I like the diversity that comes with working with various types of clients, ranging from corporations, small companies, and health care professionals to individual business owners and students. I also love the flexibility of having a broad spectrum of project types to choose from every time I sit down at my desk to work. If I don't feel particularly inspired and creative, I can put aside newsletter development for one client and instead handle a routine database development project or mail-merge a few hundred letters for another client. If my creative juices are really flowing, I can do back-to-back writing— a resume for a client, an article for my own company's newsletter, a marketing letter in response to a prospect call I received yesterday, minutes from a meeting I attended a few nights ago, a preliminary brochure design for a new client, or maybe a story to submit for possible publication in a magazine. If I have an especially high energy level and it's during a period of time when there's a low volume of telephone interruptions (11:00 P.M. or 5:30 A.M. are particularly good times for this!), I'll tackle transcription of a meeting in which there are many unidentified speakers and lots of background noise . . . or transcription from a doctor using extensive technical terminology. Were I to specialize in transcription *only*, however, I can safely say that there are days and times of the day when I would not feel inspired to tackle that kind of work, especially day after day after day.

Each secretarial service owner must establish the prototype of his or her own business service offerings. This will be dictated by market niche and need, interest, expertise, and price. Why price? Let's move into the next section, Establishing a Price Structure.

Establishing a Price Structure

How you price certain offerings will in large part determine how much of a particular type of work you want to handle. Let's use the transcription example again. In my own case, while I handle transcription on a fairly regular basis for some of my clients for whom I provide lots of *other* services, I don't actively seek just transcription work alone with any given client. I don't price that particular product with any special discounts or promotional offers, as it's not in the area of creative editorial work that I vastly prefer. A service offering transcription services exclusively would probably offer all three varieties (standard, mini- and microcassette; I don't offer mini, just standard and micro); pricing would probably be very competitive (e.g., transcription in the medical world is usually priced by the line, the word, or the character, although there is an industry move to change this). My pricing for transcription follows the same method I use for any other word processing service—an hourly charge based on the actual time expended.

There are no hard-and-fast rules for establishing specific pricing, but there are some general guidelines to consider. First and foremost, *fairly* and *reasonably* price your services so that *you* make a profit. Many home-based businesspeople underprice themselves; while it's true that your overhead is significantly less than that of an office suite or center-of-town business office location, you will most likely be providing additional conveniences to your clients (via early A.M. or late P.M. drop-off and pickup privileges, weekend appointments, etc.). Most important is that you want to be able to make a good salary, for you will undoubtedly be working harder (and enjoying it more) than you ever have before. Finally, you need to ensure a reasonable profit for yourself so that you can *stay* in business.

Refer to your initial analysis of your competition and develop a matrix of various service offerings you plan to provide. A good rule of thumb in starting out is (1) not to charge the lowest prices (unless you're really going after volume and plan to advertise that fact heavily—something most home-based entrepreneurs aren't in a position to do immediately, particularly if they're mothers with small children) and (2) not to have the highest prices (unless you're in a specialty niche area with no competition).

If you strike a balance between what's already being charged across your market area, you should have a good starting point. With regard to an hourly rate for word processing services, for example (probably the biggest cost center starting out), you should try to obtain pricing from at least ten competitors across your geographic area (including both home-based and office- or suite-based, if known/suspected). Total these ten hourly rates and divide by ten to obtain the average. This is a good double check that the amount you're planning to charge on an hourly basis won't cause sticker-shock or be too underpriced for your market.

Depending on your geographic area of the country, you'll find there are different ways of charging for your services. The two most common methods are by the hour (utilizing tenth-of-an-hour increments) and by the page (usually based on double-spaced text). With the exception of certain flat fees (e.g., resumes—a flat dollar amount for a one-page typed resume and an uplift for the second page, not counting editorial or consultation time), charging on the basis of time is probably the fairest and most equitable manner of pricing for both you and your clients. It makes allowances for quality of input as well as complexity of project. One client's "basic document to be word-processed" could be significantly more involved (complicated tables requiring you to perform calculations) and difficult to read (smudged, very light pencil-written pages on both sides) than another client's.

You can count on being asked to provide an estimate over the telephone during initial client inquiries. You probably won't encourage business by choosing not to respond to these questions. By quoting estimates on the telephone ("I charge $XX per hour in tenth-of-an-hour increments; I can typically produce seven to nine double-spaced, proofread pages per hour, averaging $XX per page"), you can give a prospective client an *idea* of a per-page rate for comparison shopping. Always reiterate that the charge is calculated on the basis of the actual time to handle the work and that you can provide a more accurate estimate once you have inspected the incoming work. It's also good to mention your typing speed (providing it is fast, more than 80 or so words per minute), but mention too that the quality of incoming documents and materials varies considerably. Always stress, "I can work with any materials, however."

When determining your rates, you need to factor in hidden costs, such as electricity and heat, a portion of your mortgage or rent for space in your home, and your costs for equipment, software, supplies and advertising, *plus* your time, experience, and expertise! There are some good industry standards available through the NASS that are useful for establishing pricing, estimating, and factoring in your speed, skill level, and years of experience (see Appendix). Nothing, however, is better than your time and experience in this business for analyzing and assessing your rates, providing quotations, and understanding what works best for you.

The following exercise helps to outline all the variables you should consider in determining the correct minimum rate you should charge. Keep in mind too that you, as the business owner, are not necessarily locking in to any of these rates (unless you sign a contract or promise a client a given rate for a fixed period of time). You are free to raise (or lower!) them at any time, as well as offer discounts and promotions whenever you choose. Remember, though, that raising your rates is something that should be approached with caution and awareness of timing. Obviously, you won't build a lot of client goodwill if your rates are going up every other month. It makes sense not to raise your rates any more frequently than once a year. During times of economic recession, service providers in many industries wait even longer than the typical year to "raise rates." You can advertise this fact if you choose to hold your rates flat over a period of a few years. This may not necessarily be in your best financial interest; you will need to continually invest resources in your growing business, and one way to do so is to increase profitability—most easily accomplished by a reasonable increase in rates at reasonable intervals of time.

Pricing Exercise

To arrive at the appropriate rate to charge, you must consider three basic variables: your expenses, your available time/billable hours, and your desired profit.

Expenses

First, assess all of your expenses. Fill in the actual or approximate *annualized* numbers for each category on the sample expense sheet (a key follows, providing more detailed instructions for all footnoted items). You will obviously need to estimate some of these numbers.

Billable Hours

After reaching an annual estimate for expenses for your business, you can then consider the amount of hours you intend or would like to work each year (and, from this, the amount of that time you can reasonably "sell"). If you plan to work forty hours a week and have three weeks of vacation per year, you would be projecting a maximum of 1,960 hours available. The amount of time you could actually expect to be compensated for, however, is considerably less than this amount. Why? Most business experts state that organized, productive entrepreneurs are doing well to be billing 60 percent of their total working time (in other words, of the 1,960 hours available, 1,176 of them could be considered "billable").

What this essentially means is that in any given forty-hour week, you will realistically be spending 25 percent (or possibly more) of your time doing nonbillable work. Every time you answer the phone, the "clock stops ticking" on a project you may have been working on but had to interrupt to answer the telephone. You may spend ten or fifteen minutes on this telephone call responding to a prospective client's inquiries about your services, scheduling an appointment, and providing directions. That is "overhead" time that cannot be charged back to any one client;

Sample Expense Sheet

Your salary[1]	$20,840.00
Utilities/house expenses[2]	300.00
Equipment[3]	1,000.00
Software[4]	300.00
Telephone/Yellow Pages advertising	1,800.00
Fax line (if separate)	-0-
Other advertising/marketing/newsletter	400.00
Professional subscription costs	100.00
Professional membership costs	150.00
Printing expenses	200.00
Office supplies and materials	800.00
Postage	300.00
Professional fees[5]	200.00
Self-employment taxes and federal and state taxes[6]	4,760.00
Shipping/overnight delivery	200.00
TOTAL ANTICIPATED ANNUAL COSTS	$31,350.00

Sample Expense Sheet

Your salary [1] $ _____

Utilities/house expenses [2]   _____

Equipment [3]   _____

Software [4]   _____

Telephone/Yellow Pages advertising   _____

Fax line (if separate)   _____

Other advertising/marketing/newsletter   _____

Professional subscription costs   _____

Professional membership costs   _____

Printing expenses   _____

Office supplies and materials   _____

Postage   _____

Professional fees [5]   _____

Self-employment taxes and federal and state taxes [6]   _____

Shipping/overnight delivery   _____

_____

TOTAL ANTICIPATED ANNUAL COSTS $ _____

[1] For a starting point, begin with the salary you'd *like* to earn. You can adjust upward or downward later on in the exercise.

[2] Determine the percentage of space your office uses as compared with the total square footage of your home available. Let's assume your office comprises 10 percent of the total area. Calculate your electrical bill for the year and then use 10 percent as that portion which your business should pay. If your electrical bill for the year totals $1,000, the portion to be assumed by your business is $100 for the year. In this example, because of the equipment you will be using, the percentage used may actually be higher; as you track your electrical bills in the first year of business, you may want to adjust this percentage upward to cover the "real" amount (perhaps 20 percent or even 25 percent for this utility).

Then, if you heat by oil or gas, take the same 10 percent amount of the annual bill and add this to the equation. If your heating costs are $500 for the year for your entire home, then $50 is the amount to be charged to your business. Don't forget to include the same percentage of any ancillary household services and expenses, including snow plowing (if you live in a section of the country for which this is relevant), lawn maintenance, trash removal, household cleaning, homeowner's insurance (provided you don't have a separate business policy or a rider to your homeowner's policy, in which case the entire amount for a business policy would be added in), security/alarm system, etc. When you take 10 percent of each of these items and add them all together, this number becomes the amount to include on this line item in the formula.

Note: Not all of these expenses are necessarily tax-deductible business expenses (always consult with a representative of the Internal Revenue Service, refer to the appropriate publications of the IRS [see Bibliography], or review with your accountant, if you have one); however, they can be considered, for purposes of your pricing formula, relevant to the overall cost of doing business.

[3] Use the depreciation tables of the IRS schedules to arrive at the appropriate number to use for this line item (for most electronic/computer equipment, three years is probably the maximum amount of time recommended, even though you may keep a piece of equipment in service beyond that time). You should always be planning for replacement costs. For instance, if you already own a computer, you may be tempted not to include an amount for this line item. This would be a mistake because in probably the next two to four years, you will want to replace your computer with a more up-to-date system—and even if you lack the desire or discipline to be saving in advance for that expenditure, your overall pricing should reflect a certain amount to be allocated to the replacement of equipment.

[4] You should allocate a certain amount of money for the purchase of new or updated software each year.

[5] Professional fees would be the services of an accountant and/or an attorney if you've decided to engage such assistance.

[6] As a general guideline, self-employment taxes will run about 13 percent, federal/state will vary, but anticipate another 10–20 percent (here is where an accounting professional specializing in small business can provide valuable assistance in your first year).

however, this type of downtime must be accounted for in your overall rates.

When you make your daily or weekly trip to the post office for replenishing supplies, to the bank for making deposits, to a client site for picking up or delivering work (providing you're not charging separately for this time), or to the office supply store for purchasing office supplies, you are expending time related to your business that cannot be billed to a client. Using a round number of $20 an hour, for example, you can quickly see that to cover your 25 percent downtime that's nonbillable, you really will be making only $15 an hour (and this doesn't take into account all of your other expenses).

For purposes of this formula, I'll use the above example a little bit later and then revise it several different ways to illustrate what can happen with just a few minor adjustments.

Profit

While many entrepreneurs in this field are happy with whatever is left over after paying all their expenses, it is smart planning to forecast, price for, and anticipate a reasonable profit. This amount could be a sum you decide to allocate to an individual retirement account, for example, or place in some other nest egg. This number is over and above the amount you've established as your salary in the expense portion of the exercise. We'll use $5,000 for the example. The number you arrive at is contingent on many factors and is also reflective of your initial reasons and goals for establishing a business. For many people being in business for themselves brings its own rewards that don't always carry a dollar value. This book has assumed throughout, however, that as much as you will love being successfully in business for yourself, a key objective is to make money.

Calculating the Formula

The simplest and most common business equation used to reach a minimum, breakeven point (and set a baseline hourly rate) employs the three components developed above in the example:

Expenses ($31,350) + Profit ($5,000) ÷ Billable Hours (1,470) = $24.73 per hour

Using all of the factors in this equation as detailed in the example, this says that $24.73 is the *minimum* amount you can charge per hour and cover all of your expenses *and* your salary and profit objectives. There are some important factors to take into account when starting a business. It is unlikely that you will start off working full-time immediately and billing thirty hours out of every forty-hour workweek. Even in an established, five-year-old business, for example, there are swings on a week-to-week basis. It is also highly unusual (but not impossible) for a start-up business to *turn a profit* in its first year. In other words, while it is reasonable to hope to earn a salary (again, not that common in a start-up business) in your first year of doing business, it may not be possible to provide for a profit. In addition, during your first year of establishing a business you will probably need to inject a substantial amount of money (quite typically your own funds) in purchasing equipment and software you may not already own (a bonus if you do) and investing in "extra" forms of advertising (covered earlier) while waiting for your Yellow Pages advertising to appear in a new directory. You will *save*, though, on your telephone bill because the charge for the Yellow Pages advertising will not appear until the month the new directory containing your ads is published. Tax obligations are less as well, if your earnings are less than estimated.

Now, let's have some fun playing with the variables to see what happens. If you decide that a goal of owning your own business is to work fewer hours than you might have in a more traditional setting but still earn the same compensation, let's cut back by 50 percent of the billable hours to see what happens.

Expenses ($31,350) + Profit ($5,000) ÷ Billable Hours (735) = $49.46 per hour

Realistic? Probably not. But, you might determine that while you can't expect to earn the same amount in half the time, you *can* compromise with a cutback in projected profit to perhaps $2,500, a slight decrease in compensation to $17,000, and work thirty hours a week (thus billing 22.5 hours using the 75 percent calculation). Run the equation again (remember to adjust the tax line item as well).

Expenses ($27,510) + Profit ($2,500) ÷ Billable Hours (1,102.5) = $27.22 per hour

That's probably more reasonable! Experiment with the equation to assess the impact of any decision. As a final step in the exercise, compare this information as you are calculating with the competitive information for your market that you ascertained earlier. If you find that the hourly minimum you've determined in this exercise falls somewhere along the line you established for your competitors, you can confirm your placement on the scale. If you find that your minimum is way below the scale, then move the number up (total "profit" at this point!) to be more reasonable. If you are significantly above the competitor who charges the most, you might consider reassessing why your numbers look so high: Is it because you are projecting spending too much in the first year on equipment? (Maybe consider leasing in the first year only.) Are you anticipating too high a profit for a first-year business start-up? Or is your strategy to be the most expensive and provide the best service . . . and will your advertising reflect this stance? There's nothing wrong with being the most expensive, provided that you are patient, willing to work harder at bringing in first-time clients, and have the necessary reserves to fund a probable slower start-up. There are hidden perceptions to pricing: For some, higher price means higher quality. If you pitch to that belief, you may find a successful niche. This is not recommended, however, as the way to get a business going successfully in the quickest way possible. Striking a median position along the scale for your marketplace (while at the same time ensuring that your minimum costs to break even are covered, still yielding you a fair salary and a reasonable profit) makes the most sense for starting out successfully.

The following form illustrates a professional way to simply announce future price increases to your client base. Never apologize for increasing your rates.

Sample Notice to Announce Price Changes/Increases

Company Name _____

Address/Telephone _____

Please be advised that the following prices will become effective
January 1,* _____:

Word Processing Services—$XX/hour

Desktop Publishing Services—$XX/hour

Editorial/Consultation Services—$XX/hour

Administrative Services—$XX/hour

Minimum Charge—.5 hour at prevailing service rate

[Also mention any change in pricing for ancillary services: stationery, copies, fax, notarizing, etc.]

We appreciate your business and thank you for the opportunity to provide professional services. [Include business slogan.]

*Keep in mind that rate increases do not necessarily have to be the first of the year.

A small, laserprinted postcard is an efficient way to communicate price changes to regular clients; for clients you haven't seen in three or more months, price change notification is probably not necessary (the next time they contact you for a quote on a project, you'll simply quote at the rates in place at that time).

Credit

Credit, particularly for a new business, should be extended judiciously. For those clients seeking to have you carry them "on account," an application should be completed (see following sample). With individual clients, their word and your mutual agreement are probably sufficient.

You will typically find that most medical practices, large companies, and corporations will pay your invoices according to their internal accounts payable policies (usually thirty days, sometimes forty-five days). With smaller accounts, generally individual business owners who utilize your services on a regular basis, you should discuss whatever terms seem most appropriate. The majority that want billing "on account" will expect to be invoiced once per month and have terms of anywhere between ten and thirty days. Attempt to stagger the billing dates of these monthly accounts so that you have an even division between those you bill at the end of the month and those that you bill on the fifteenth of the month. Why? *Cash flow.* One of the most important factors of any viable business that succeeds is appropriate cash flow. If you find that the majority of your regular, ongoing business is made up of monthly accounts all billing at the end of the month (and all paying, e.g., at thirty days), you're going to experience cash shortages the first two or three weeks of each month. If you stagger your billing cycle (simply in half), those accounts billed on the fifteenth paying at thirty days will provide an injection of cash at the middle of every month and those accounts billed on the thirtieth paying at thirty days will give the cash boost at the end of every subsequent month.

For extremely regular accounts where you're providing in excess of ten or fifteen hours of service per week, week in and week out, you may want to consider billing twice a month; for accounts this active it's a good idea to establish terms at net ten days (vs. thirty). In fact, I recommend at least establishing your terms as "net ten days" on all accounts. Consider it this way: If a client first utilizes your services on May 1 and then continues to use services throughout the month, by the time you generate the invoice on May 31, you may be billing $1,000 (for purposes of this example). If the client takes thirty days to pay this invoice, you won't receive a check until perhaps June 30 or even the first week in July (almost two months after first providing the service). If you bill the client twice a month, that shortens your receipt cycle by at least two weeks, plus provides cash injections on a steady every-other-week basis thereafter.

Sample Credit Application

CREATIVE SECRETARIAL SERVICES

P.O. Box 111 • Anytown, USA 55555
(333) 777–2222 • Fax (333) 777–6666

CREDIT APPLICATION

Client Name _____ Title _____

Company _____

Address _____

Mailing Address (if Different) _____

City _____ State _____ Zip Code _____

Telephone (Area Code) _____ (Number) _____

Fax (Area Code) _____ (Number) _____

Type of Business _____ Years in Business _____

Number of Employees at Your Location _____

Dun & Bradstreet Number (if any) _____

Do you use a purchase order system? YES ___ NO ___

BANK REFERENCES

1. Financial Institution _____

Address _____ _____

City _____ State _____ Zip Code _____

Telephone (Area Code) _____ (Number) _____

Fax (Area Code) _____ (Number) _____

Business Checking Account Number _____

Person to Contact at Bank _____

2. Financial Institution _____

Address _____ _____

City _____ State _____ Zip Code _____

Telephone (Area Code) _____ (Number) _____

Fax (Area Code) _____ (Number) _____

Business Checking Account Number _____

Person to Contact at Bank _____

THE VERY BEST IN BUSINESS SUPPORT SERVICES!

CREDIT REFERENCES

1. Company Name _____
Address _____
City _____ State _____ Zip Code _____
Telephone (Area Code) _____ (Number) _____
Fax (Area Code) _____ (Number) _____
Account Number _____
Person to Contact/Title_____

2. Company Name _____
Address _____
City _____ State _____ Zip Code _____
Telephone (Area Code) _____ (Number) _____
Fax (Area Code) _____ (Number) _____
Account Number _____
Person to Contact/Title_____

3. Company Name _____
Address _____
City _____ State _____ Zip Code _____
Telephone (Area Code) _____ (Number) _____
Fax (Area Code) _____ (Number) _____
Account Number _____
Person to Contact/Title_____

MUST BE SIGNED BY AUTHORIZED COMPANY OFFICER

I certify that all statements made by me in this application are for the purpose of obtaining credit and are correct to my knowledge. I authorize these references to release my credit status and to provide such other information as Creative Secretarial Services may require. The undersigned expressly agrees to make payment in full to Creative Secretarial Services for all purchases in accordance with Creative Secretarial Services invoice(s). At the discretion of Creative Secretarial Services, a deposit/project retainer may be required in advance of commencing work on a project. Applicant acknowledges that all accounts over ten (10) days old will be assessed a service charge at the maximum rate permitted by law. The undersigned agrees to pay a reasonable attorney's fee and all other costs and expenses incurred by Creative Secretarial Services in the collection of any obligation of the undersigned pursuant hereto. This application for credit, once accepted by Creative Secretarial Services, shall become part of every invoice to applicant and is incorporated herein. This application shall remain Creative Secretarial Services' property whether or not it is accepted and approved.

Signature _____ Title _____

Date _____

Credit Department Use Only

Date Application Received _____ Date Application Approved _____

Invoicing

Your invoices should include terms (whether "payable upon completion of a project" or "net due ten days from date of invoice"). If a client is tax-exempt (in a state where you are otherwise required to collect sales tax), the tax exemption number should be noted on the invoice. If you are handling work for a reseller (i.e., a printing company), the reseller should provide you with a copy of a resale certificate onto which their sales and use tax registration number appears; you do not collect sales tax on this work because the reseller will be incorporating your charges in *their* invoicing and collecting sales tax from their customer. If a client is with a corporation that uses a purchase order system (this should be ascertained upon acceptance of the first project), be certain to reference the appropriate purchase order number. If a client requires that your invoices bear numbers, you should develop a numbering system within the invoice template on your computer, unless you use an invoice program that generates numbers automatically. A simple system I use for those clients requiring it is B94•03; the *B* denotes the first letter of the corporate name (e.g., Brown Corporation), the *94* is for the year in which the invoice period occurs, and the *03* indicates this is the third invoice I've generated for this client in a given year. Because the invoice is also dated, there should never be a duplication. I've never had more than about a half-dozen clients at any one point that required an invoice number on their invoices, so this easy-to-use method works well.

Recordkeeping

Depending on your computer software, you may wish to try one of the many good bookkeeping/accounting packages (Dollars + Sense and Quicken are both good programs in the Mac world). While an accountant can set up books for you to follow if you so choose, you'll readily find a plethora of good information in your public library as well as through the Small Business Administration (see the Appendix).

Sample Invoice

Allen's Secretarial Service

123 Main Street
Anywhere, USA 89888
(444) 444–4444 • Fax (444) 444–3333

Invoice for Services Rendered   Date: _____

Company Name   Purchase Order #_____

Address

Invoice # _____   Billing Contact: _____

Date of Service	Project Description	Hours/Rate @ $XX.00	Subtotal

Payment is due upon completion of project.   Subtotal $

Sales Tax $

Total $

Professional Secretarial and Office Support Services

Whatever method you develop, attempt to keep it as simple and easy to use as possible—once your business really begins to be *busy*, you won't want to spend precious time on complicated entry tasks. Your goal with recordkeeping should be twofold: (1) to provide timely information for managing your business and understanding its cyclic peaks and areas for growth and (2) to provide accurate reporting information for city, state, and government agencies and filing of tax returns.

In addition to maintaining financial forms (discussed in chapter 3) tracking my company's financial health, I record vital client information about two additional business areas, using a program in Dollars + Sense. This can be done in a number of other accounting programs as well as set up on a spreadsheet program such as Excel or Lotus.

Client Tracker

The Client Tracker form I have developed records on a monthly basis all billing to each client account. This information is pulled from the invoices that make up the AR (accounts receivable) Log discussed in the next section. For some clients there is just one monthly invoice generated. For other clients an invoice is prepared with completion of each project throughout the course of the month (so that there might be eight to twelve invoices for an active client). All corporate and individual business accounts are itemized in the client tracker. I find it useful to bulk together some categories; for example, resume clientele are grouped together for a month, as are those clients requiring preparation of term papers. I don't find it particularly valuable to review a Client Tracker and see thirty or forty different proper names individually listed (that's about how many resume clients I see each month). Instead, I like to group that number together to see what the overall number is as a percentage of my total business.

The format I have set up for a Client Tracker provides month-to-month information, quarterly subtotals, and annual numbers. In addition, when the archiving function is applied at year's end, the information then becomes available for reference in the subsequent year. In other words, at a glance I can tell where my biggest client is this year and how the numbers compare with those of last year (and of the year before). I always chart the information graphically, as well, at the end of each month, to see at a glance where my clients rank as a percentage of my business. The old 80-20 rule almost always applies: That is, you can expect 80 percent of your revenues to come from 20 percent of your base. Apply to this some good common sense for running a successful business: Those clients comprising the 20 percent of your base that yields 80 percent of your revenues should be your top priority and receive your consistent attention. By tracking numbers in this manner, you can quickly spot downward trends and attempt to reverse them.

For example, if you note that one of your top clients over the past year begins to have a downward spiral in terms of generating less and less work from month to month, you might want to inquire as to the reason. It may be a perfectly natural business cycle, but it might represent an opportunity for you to provide enhanced services or address a problem you might otherwise not have known existed. By watching your numbers on a regular basis, you will also observe those once infrequent clients spending more time—and money—with you. These may be the next "stars" on your top 20 percent list and deserve extra attention as you cultivate their business!

Sample Client Tracker
(For the six-month period January–June, 19____)

Client Name	Jan.	Feb.	Mar.	Apr.	May	June

Cost Tracker

The Cost Tracker format I have established takes the same information used to develop the Client Tracker, but instead of recording it by account name, the information provided on each invoice is keyed in by various cost centers. For instance, if your largest account is ABC Company and its monthly invoice amount is $1,271.02, the invoice will detail how this amount was derived (this is a fairly typical itemization for an account's invoice). Let's use the following example to break it out (all fictitious numbers):

3 hours of editorial services @ $75/hour	$ 225.00
5 hours of desktop publishing @ $65/hour	325.00
5 hours of word processing @ $50/hour	250.00
Office supplies (Pentaflex file folders, manila file folders, and labels to complete "Smith" project)	75.00
Postage for "Jones" mailing	58.00
FEDEX charges (7 @ $22.50)	157.50
Special pickup at airport (flat fee)	50.00
Fax charges	70.00
SUBTOTAL	**$ 1,210.50**
Sales Tax (assuming it's 5 percent)	60.53
TOTAL	**$ 1,271.03**

In recording this information to the Cost Tracker, hourly rate categories are separated and the respective amounts are entered under each category. Each of the other entries has its own category—office supplies, fax charges, delivery charges, miscellaneous (e.g., for the special airport pickup, which is not a commonly billed service), postage, and so forth. Once all invoices have been broken out into these respective categories and totaled for the month, you will have an excellent picture as to where your time is spent (vis-à-vis the different hourly categories) and where you are selling additional services. Some items may be strictly "pass-alongs" to your clients (i.e., you may choose not to add any extra charges for providing overnight delivery; e.g., the company you select charges $22.50 for an overnight letter and you pass this cost to your client without adding any additional markup) and therefore not represent any profit to you. Other items may be nearly "pure" profit (if you charge clients to receive faxes, once you have absorbed the cost of the machine and separate telephone line, if applicable, your only cost to receive faxes is the paper charge; this can be highly profitable).

Most secretarial services add on a small amount for ancillary services to cover their time in handling them. Use of overnight services is a good example. While clients might choose to make their own arrangements, for their convenience you handle complete arrangements, from telephoning for a pickup and completing the accompanying shipping document (which requires you to maintain an adequate supply of materials, provided at no cost by the various shipping companies) to wrapping a package securely and presenting the package to the delivery service person when he or she arrives at your office later in the day. All of this takes time on your part—and it's reasonable to add a small markup for this service (perhaps $2.00–$5.00) to the actual cost charged by the shipping company before passing it along to your client.

Using the Cost Tracker on a month-to-month basis is valuable in terms of spotting trends in the way your business is growing. If you experiment with offering a new service, for example, editorial services, at a higher hourly rate than your word processing services (which it should be), you can observe how this category of business is growing from month to month. If you determine that it is well-received in your market area, you may opt to concentrate more time and resources in further advertising and developing this segment of your business. The flip side would be a decision to offer transcription services keyed at a different hourly rate from your word processing rate (even if only a $1.00 difference). Let's suppose you take a separate Yellow Pages ad under Transcription Services for a year and track an hourly rate of $22 (for purposes of this example, we'll say $22 as compared with $20 for your regular word processing rate). By using a form similar to the Cost Tracker to view activity for the twelve months your advertising has appeared in the Yellow Pages under this new category, you may note that your billing was zero for the first two months (June and July); $50 a month for August, September, and October; zero again in November; $75 in December; and $25 for each month January through May. If your additional advertising expense in the Yellow Pages is $40 per month for this ad, it would be a reasonable conclusion that this is not a viable profit center *unless* you choose to do something different. This might be analysis of your competition to discover that *their* hourly rate for this service is only $18 (hence, you are overpricing for this service, something you should have checked before determining to offer transcription services). It might also be that you can assess from your different clients in this area a potential surge of business coming in the next year. Engage in open discussion with these clients. Let them know you are considering specializing in this area—are they willing (or likely) to provide additional business? Is additional business even available? Are they growing in this direction? All of these factors can influence whether or not you spend even more money advertising this service the following year—or pull your ad out of the book and not seek to further develop this area of business.

Sample Cost Tracker
(For the month   , 19____)

$20/hr.	$22/hr.	$25/hr.	$28/hr.	$30/hr.	$35/hr.	Copies	Fax	Supplies	Postage	FEDEX

(usually a two- or three-page form for a given month, with all cost center categories running along the top of each page)

Managing Accounts Receivable

With individuals you should collect payment upon completion of a project at the time of pickup. Depending on your own philosophy, you may wish to establish a cash-only policy or determine that personal checks are acceptable. It's always a good idea to collect a deposit (usually 50 percent) up front when a project is first delivered to you (again, from first-time, individual clients, especially students and resume clientele); with established clients this shouldn't be necessary.

You may want to investigate offering clients the option of paying by credit card (Visa or MasterCard). It is costly, however (initial fees of up to $200, plus a percentage of each sale, usually between 3 and 7 percent), and many banks frown upon offering this through new home-based businesses. If you decide that the protection of not getting bounced checks is worth the cost of providing this option, you may wish to check with an independent sales organization (ISO) for assistance in obtaining merchant status. These businesses exist to help other businesses apply for accounts, and they charge a fee on top of whatever the bank would normally charge you. Information regarding ISOs can be located in the Bibliography section of the Appendix.

If you determine that offering the option to clients of charging to a major credit card makes sense for your business, you might wish to structure your pricing to provide a discount to those clients paying cash, as it is not permissible by law to add a surcharge for use of a credit card.

Many secretarial services, including my own, accept personal checks; however, you must be especially careful when taking checks from transient clients—that is, clients you may see one time only. You obviously want to limit your exposure to bounced checks as much as possible. Unfortunately, it is the rare secretarial service (or any business, for that matter) that hasn't been the recipient of a bounced check at least once or twice.

If you are working with a client that after a few months has the potential of being a "regular" (most sought after, naturally!), you might want to extend credit over the course of the month using a log to record time on that client's projects on an ongoing basis (see the Client Production Schedule earlier in this chapter). A summary invoice is prepared at the end of the billing period. Establish payment expectations with a client at the onset (e.g., that billing will occur once monthly, with payment due within ten days of receipt of your invoice).

It's also a good idea to have the client initial each entry on the log as completed work is picked up throughout the month.

How you track your ARs will partially be a function of how you establish your books and how you like to organize your files. I utilize a very basic and easy-to-follow system, detailed below.

As I invoice clients throughout the month, I provide them with a hard copy of the original invoice and file a copy in their project file as well as in a chronological file folder located at my desk. On a regular basis (every week or so), I take the chronological file folder and enter the key information onto an AR Log I maintain in a large notebook. Once "posted," the invoice copy is placed in the notebook under the appropriate month in chronological order. As payments are received, the AR Log is updated with payment date and amount (I don't bother to check the amount/date paid on the actual invoice copy in the book, as the log serves as the "Bible").

When I am preparing my bank deposit (I generally make deposits every day or every other day—I'm always anxious to deposit personal checks in the event there might be a problem with a given check clearing), I enter in my check register each individual check amount and client name, as well as the total amount of the deposit and date. For example, a typical recording of a deposit in my check register might look like this:

2/17   Jones $100.00, ABC Company $250.50,   + $800.50
        Smith $300.00, Edwards Corp. $150.00

This provides a system of "checks and balances" for me and can be used to reconcile any discrepancy where I might for some reason be uncertain from looking at the AR Log whether a client has paid. When invoicing my monthly accounts, I refer to the AR Log to see if any unpaid balance should be carried forward to the next billing period. I have utilized this system for more than ten years and have never had a problem with it. I also find that this method allows me to respond immediately to clients calling to inquire about their account balance—no matter what I may be doing on the computer in another program, I can simply consult the AR Log, tell them the date and amount of their last payment, and quickly review the log to determine any outstanding invoices. Over the years I also have found that it is important to keep somewhere in your files a copy of every invoice generated for each client. Occasionally (and this is generally only with large companies), I am required to resubmit copies of actual invoices for payment in instances where staff may have changed, paperwork may have been misplaced or lost at the company, and the like. By having physical copies in my file, I don't have to recompose actual invoices in the system—and I don't need to use valuable disk space to keep the copies in a running disk file. I simply update the template invoice that appears in each client's "file" on his or her disk.

Once again, if you decide to automate your financial records and the program you utilize provides for invoicing, you may want to experiment with an automated system on your computer.

Collections

Managing collections is a necessary aspect of any business and is probably one of the more unpleasant activities in which you'll need to engage at least periodically. If you have established good credit guidelines, invoice your clients regularly, and stay on top of unpaid accounts, you shouldn't have too much difficulty. There will, however, inevitably come a time when one of the following situations occurs:

A client's check bounces. You immediately contact the client by phone upon notification from your bank that the check did not clear (usually, because of "insufficient funds," although I have had instances where an account was no longer open). You pleasantly explain to the client what happened. Always assume at the begin-

Sample AR Log

AR Log—Year: _____ Month: _____ Page: _____

Date	Amount	Date Paid	Client	Project	Source

ning that it was an honest error. Give the client a chance to apologize/explain and then ascertain a commitment for resolving the situation. Unless it is a regular client for whom this really was an honest mistake, I recommend requesting cash payment or a certified bank check for the amount due, *plus* the amount the bank charges you for the problem as well as any administrative fee you wish to add ($5.00 or $10.00 seems typical in this industry to add on to the bank's charge to cover for the inconvenience). Also, be sure to add on any amount you may be charged for checks *you* write that do not clear because of this check not clearing.

Hopefully, you're able to sustain a reasonable balance in your business checking account at any one point to provide for this occurrence. Keeping a $500 or even $1,000 cushion available at all times in your account is not a bad idea and helps to cover for situations of this type, which usually are rare. Using the Client Work Order form from the original project for which this situation has occurred, record briefly the notes of your conversation(s) held throughout the collection process. Note the date you received the bank notice and the date/time of your call to the client. Note the commitment made by the client, with a specific date. If the client does not follow through on the commitment, immediately contact the client the next day to inquire about the status, restating what the original commitment was. You will probably find that the majority of instances in this category are resolved within a week or two.

Unfortunately, there will likely be a time when either a company goes out of business before paying your invoice or an individual client moves but leaves no forwarding address and closes his or her bank account (after writing you a check that bounces). The experience of most people in this business that I've talked with is that you will have to write some business off each year; that is, chalk it up to bad business (and take it as an expense, "bad debts from sales or services," which is an expense item on Schedule C of the federal income tax form). You can attempt to obtain amounts due your business through small claims court, depending on the amount of time you have available to warrant the accompanying headaches of pursuing this action. I have found a reasonably successful method of collecting on unpaid accounts (or accounts for which checks have bounced) that costs little in terms of time or money. I initially telephone, following the steps outlined above. I record all conversations and note on my desktop appointment calendar when a commitment should occur. If it does not, I will call again, even several times.

If thirty days pass with no payment, I then briefly document the telephone calls, dates, and commitments in a letter, attaching a copy of the invoice, and formally announce in writing that "if full payment in the amount of $XX isn't received by a certain date [I give ten days at this point], legal action through small claims court will be taken." If day ten arrives with no payment, I call one last time—and then promptly mail the delinquent client a copy of the small claims court's "Small Claim and Notice of Suit" document, fully completed with the relevant facts of the case. These forms are available free of charge from the superior court in your county. I do *not* mail the form to the small claims court (which entails a filing fee of about $25 or $30). I have found that simply sending such clients the copy of the form is enough to spur many of them to pay.

Allocating Funds for Tax Obligations

As you are managing your income, expenses, and cash flow, you should establish a means for saving aside monies for your quarterly tax obligations—self-employment tax, state sales tax (if relevant in your state), and so on. If desired, an accounting professional can advise the best means for doing this, in addition to advising the proper way for reporting your income (cash or accrual basis). A simple way to ensure proper savings is to allocate on a monthly basis the appropriate percentage of all that month's business. If, for example, 5 percent is your state's sales tax percentage that you are required to collect on all sales, at the end of the month total all the taxable business you've billed, calculate the 5 percent amount, and set that aside until the quarter in which the payment is due. Likewise for self-employment, federal, and any state taxes: You should set aside a given percentage (conservatively, 25–30 percent). This may seem like a lot of money to set aside for payment of taxes, but if you don't plan for this on a regular, monthly basis, filing of quarterly returns will be difficult if not impossible.

Cultivating Client Relationships

This next aspect of "getting down to business" assumes that you have clients beginning to come to your service. Nearly every marketing publication in existence advises that it is much easier and less costly to retain a current client than it is to find a new client to take a former client's place. In addition, there is an informal rule of thumb in business today stating that a happy client will tell three to four people about your business (all prospective clients), and an unhappy client may tell ten to twelve people about your service! Therefore, it makes sense to satisfy and take good care of your valuable clients. Besides providing excellent service and quality, for which you are charging (hopefully, at the appropriate rate, having computed a reasonable and fair salary, plus profit), you should invest a small amount of time as well in going the extra mile to always thank each client for his or her business upon the conclusion of a transaction. Sending greeting cards is a thoughtful and appropriate gesture that isn't excessively costly. Instead of or in addition to communicating at Christmas, consider sending a thank-you to clients around Thanksgiving—to thank them for being your clients. You can use other seasonal events to create a theme for client communications: Valentine's Day (to let clients know how much you "love" the opportunity of providing professional services to them) and April Fool's Day (to tell your clients they're "the best—*no foolin'!*"), for example.

Developing a newsletter for your business (discussed fully in chapter 4) is an excellent way to subtly keep your company's name in front of regular and occasional clients as well as prospective clients. It also can effectively advertise the newsletter writing/production service you offer. The format can be as simple as a one-page, three-panel self-mailer. A quarterly or bimonthly schedule is usually manageable and affordable. It's also an ideal vehicle for spotlighting new products or services you may be adding as well as demonstrating your skill and expertise in writing, layout, and design. My clients repeatedly tell me how much they enjoy my newsletter—from reading my chatty column to finding helpful tips they can use in their own business pursuits.

Managing client relationships successfully and effectively is an important skill for any business owner. When you're in a business providing strictly services, as obviously is the case with a secretarial service, clients primarily will do business with you *because* of you. While price, location, or an initial satisfaction of their need for a particular service may have attracted them to you in the first place, repeat client business will be a function of how well you serve your clients' perceived and actual needs. What do I mean by this? Let's say a client contacts you to prepare a small mail-merge project of twenty-five names. You are given the responsibility of typesetting a cover letter (handwritten reasonably well by the client), creating the small base of twenty-five names and addresses from various newspaper and telephone directory clippings, and printing individual letters and matching envelopes. Not a big deal—maybe, all told, one hour's worth of work or so. But this is the first time that this client has contacted you. So what can you do "above and beyond" to help pave the way for future business with this client?

When typesetting the letter, objectively consider the message being delivered. Can you offer any suggestions on how to improve the language chosen, the way in which the message is delivered, the use of a dynamic opening or dramatic close, the use of an effective eyebrow? An eyebrow is the use of a short, distinctive phrase— placed above the salutation—that is created to capture the reader's attention. It is typically set in a larger font size than the body of the letter, is usually in boldface, and is frequently set in a different font from the body of the letter. An eyebrow replaces the more conventional subject line, or "RE" line, on a cover letter. For a company marketing a new service that promises to save its client companies money, an effective eyebrow might be: "Our Company Is in the

Business of Saving Companies *Like Yours* Big Bucks." See the following example.

XYZ Company
123 Main Street • Your City, USA 55555
(800) 343–3434

Date

Addressee

Title

Company

Address

City, State, Zip

Our Company Is in the Business of Saving Companies *Like Yours* Big Bucks.

Dear _____:

I'll bet that captured your attention . . . want to learn more about how XYZ Company can save your firm a substantial amount of money . . . (etc.)

Merely making well-considered recommendations to a client demonstrates that the client is not dealing with just a typing clerk but a professional committed to the success of his or her business. This type of "team thinking" provides comfort *and* confidence to clients in cultivating an attitude of caring about their own work. Clients begin to see you as a business partner, someone who is really working on their side to help them achieve their goals. As your opinions become valued, clients will turn to you more and more for advice on matters ranging from how best to write a sales letter to how a proposal can be effectively developed. Once you demonstrate your expertise in "thinking like a business partner," your advice will be sought in other areas and on other projects. This many times leads to additional projects . . . often coming from suggestions you might have made. For the large numbers of individual small-business owners throughout the United States who utilize secretarial and office support services, there are literally hundreds of opportunities for suggesting add-on projects. There is hardly a businessperson who couldn't benefit from a well-developed brochure or newsletter. Most simply lack the time and expertise to develop their own . . . or, even more likely, haven't considered what such a piece could accomplish for their business.

As the provider of professional secretarial and office support services, you are in a unique position to deliver many ancillary services to your client base beyond the obvious word processing projects. Use your expertise and captivated client base to your advantage—open new profit centers and sell add-on services to your regular clients that will truly benefit from them. A significant by-product is the higher rate you can—and should—charge for such creative work.

Organizations/Affiliations . . . Developing a Community Network

A membership in both the National Association of Secretarial Services and its local chapter in your county or state is highly recommended, especially at the local level, if you have a strong chapter (see the Appendix), and particularly during the start-up phase of operating your business. You'll have an opportunity to network with others experiencing some of the same challenges as you—acquiring clients, getting repeat business, and effectively managing a business from your home (although many members are based in retail offices or executive suites, a number are home-based). You can benefit from the experiences of others as well as possibly develop a referral network for overflow work. This can work both ways: In the start-up phase, you'll most likely be hoping to obtain overflow from someone else's business, but as your business grows, you will appreciate having cultivated a network of professionals to whom you can confidently refer client projects you simply lack the time for . . . or whom you can contact for assistance in a possible subcontractor arrangement.

Depending on the fees required, consider joining your local chapter of the chamber of commerce and/or the Better Business Bureau. The chamber typically provides many opportunities for professional networking and gaining visibility in your community. As with membership in any professional association or organization, you must be willing to share your time and expertise with others in order to reap some of the advantages of belonging to such a group. The Better Business Bureau doesn't usually offer the monthly forums for meeting that the chamber does, but some business owners find it useful to pay the hefty annual fee (usually, around $300) to have their name registered. For women, investigate local chapters of various businesswomen's entrepreneurial groups (local universities and, once again, the chamber of commerce can be good sources for checking out the existence of these groups). If no targeted group exists in your community, consider starting an informal organization yourself. It's a great way to gain publicity and build worthwhile professional contacts at the same time.

Seminars and programs offered by the Small Business Administration, local colleges, and businesses such as the telephone company provide excellent opportunities to enhance your knowledge in specifically targeted areas as well as meet with other professionals. Check into and take advantage of low-cost, day-long conferences offered in your region. The SBA frequently collaborates with other businesses to produce top-notch programs where you can further hone marketing skills and meet others in similar businesses. Don't overlook programs made available by your chamber of commerce and chapters of professional organizations.

6
Running a Home-based Business...and a Household

For many home-based operators of desktop publishing, typing, and word processing services, the lure into this field of work is the ability to *be* home-based and thus manage the multiple responsibilities of earning an income—often while being available to one's children. I wouldn't be totally honest were I to say that it's easy to run a home-based business with small children—but it is possible and it's highly rewarding.

For those without children and/or empty-nesters, you'll find sprinkled throughout this section recommendations that will apply (and maybe find yourself thankful not to have small children underfoot). I've noted those sections especially applicable to individuals with small children. No matter what your circumstances, operating a home-based secretarial service will, in all likelihood, be one of the most satisfying and rewarding ventures you'll ever undertake. Among many other benefits it certainly beats the rat race of getting yourself (and possibly kids) out the door by a certain time every morning and coming home exhausted at dinner hour with groceries and a briefcase (and maybe kids in tow also) each night. As a home-based business owner, you may still find yourself exhausted at times, but the *big* difference is that *you're* in control (or you can be, if you so choose and if you possess good self-discipline).

The beauty of a home-based business is that you dictate the workload and the hours, not someone else. If you find yourself running to the beat of many demanding clients, that's a challenge for you to address; however, that's not likely to occur in the first year of starting up and operating your own business.

Here, then, are some time-proven techniques and suggestions for successfully maintaining a profitable home-based business that doesn't infringe *too* much on your family's life.

If You Have Young Children

Many home-based mothers balance their day through the use of some form of partial child care—be it an after-school high-school-age sitter for their children, part-time (and sometimes full-time) placement in nursery schools and day care centers, or summer camp programs. Keep in mind that whatever works best for you is what is important. Even if your business grows to the point where it is full time (and this is what you want) and you determine that full-time day care is appropriate, you still have the wonderful flexibility of shuffling your work schedule and client appointments when your children are ill and need to be at home or when you decide to take an impromptu day off and head to the beach with your kids or accompany them on a school field trip. This compares very favorably with a mom working full time at a company with perhaps a hectic travel schedule that keeps her away from home for days and nights at a time. If you manage to work around your children being home full-time with you, you'll still have to juggle work when they are ill and demand your complete attention all day long. But you have the option of working late at night or early in the morning (or both, during busy dissertation deadline time!) while they sleep.

Scheduling Appointments

My recommendation is to work by appointment only and not permit drop-ins. I've had several persistent clients over the years who failed, at times, to adhere to my appointment-only policy and dropped in at inconvenient times (e.g., when I was in the middle of nursing a baby). These occasional occurrences have actually provided many laughs over the years.

A little side humor here—the funniest moment in this area occurred several years ago when I was eight months pregnant with my youngest child. Although it was during February and cold and snowy in New England, *I* couldn't get cool enough or comfortable enough sleeping and found sleeping au natural to be the most convenient. Because I had not yet installed a laser printer, I was using a daisy wheel, letter-quality printer. For those of you with experience on these, you know how noisy they are when printing. I had a 200-page document (all statistical pages filled with bars, columns, numbers, etc.—lots of tiny type) to print one morning. Because I knew it would take literally hours to print and I couldn't stand the noise while it was printing, I decided to get up early and—before even showering or dressing—go get the printer started. That way, by the time the twins were up and we were out in the office area, it would perhaps be half-completed.

I dashed as quickly as an eight-months-pregnant woman can out to my desk and started up the computer (now, bear in mind, my office is of a contemporary style, surrounded by floor-to-ceiling windows, no curtains; the office is next to the garage and faces the driveway). I had just about queued the document to print when up my sidewalk, from the driveway, walks a client. It's 6:00 A.M.! I'm wearing nothing, very pregnant—and completely vulnerable, sitting surrounded by all these windows and nowhere to hide. I shouted to my husband, who came running—not to my defense but to the door! I had no alternative—I hopped into the garage.

This client, with whom I'd worked for several years, was acquainted with my husband and began what seemed like an interminably long conversation in the middle of my office about his new car. I'm standing barefooted and bare-everything-else on a cold, cement garage floor; it was no more than 20° Fahrenheit! The client finally left . . . and I think I resumed speaking to my husband sometime that afternoon. I've never chanced it again by coming into my office naked, although a big benefit every home-based business owner has is working after hours in pajamas. The *importance* of scheduled appointments . . .

By scheduling appointments, you have a luxury enjoyed by few in the corporate world of giving yourself time off when *you* want it. If you find with your schedule that you prefer doing your creative work during early morning hours, before the phones start and/or kids awaken, that's your prerogative. But unless you really want to be working twelve or so hours a day, it doesn't mean that you should write from 4:00 until 9:00 A.M. and *then* offer "conventional" business hours of 9:00 to 5:00! Likewise, if you are a night owl (as I am) and do your best work between 9:00 P.M. and 1:00 A.M., you probably don't want to be available to clients in your office at 7:30 or 8:00 A.M.

How you schedule your appointments is strictly up to you—and doesn't need to be the business of your clients. If you can meet with clients only in the mornings, for example (perhaps you have children in nursery school or kindergarten and they're home afternoons), you don't *have* to advise your clients that you can't meet with them in the afternoons "because the children are at home." Instead, as you're scheduling time, simply make morning times the only option. "Would you prefer to get together first thing in the morning or nearer to lunch?" If pushed for an afternoon appointment, simply state, "I'm completely booked afternoons this week. Would a morning later in the week work better for your schedule, or would you like an evening [or weekend] appointment?"

If you are involved in some other activity—from training for a marathon to attending classes mornings at a local university, or from serving on a committee at your children's school to volunteering with the elderly at a hospital—you have the flexibility to set your work schedule around these commitments and interests. Some secretarial service owners offer client appointments on just one or two days per week and reserve the balance of their time for handling project work without interruptions. They know that they have to "dress for business" only one or two days each week and can be entirely comfortable, productive, and free from distractions the rest of the time. Other business owners find that they are most productive in the morning; therefore, they let their answering machines pick up all morning calls and never schedule clients in the morning—instead, they meet with clients in the afternoons. The point here is simply this: It's *your* business, and you have the flexibility to create the schedule most suited to your needs at any given time. I do, however, recommend that you keep your regular clients posted of any changes. For example, when I was writing this book, I had to allocate time into my already very demanding schedule to work strictly on this project. I experimented with trying to allocate a few hours during each business day but found that client emergencies kept infringing upon that time. Then I hit upon the idea of booking the same day each week "out of the office" to write. I advised all my clients in advance, including via a brief note in my quarterly newsletter; added the information to my message on my answering machine; and scheduled accordingly. It meant the four other weekdays were more compressed than ever, with Thursday night's work inevitably spilling way into the wee hours of Friday before I could catch up on my sleep. But it worked. I had Fridays fully available to write. That same kind of scheduling discipline can be applied to any major project you might undertake—as well as be used for any personal objective you may set for yourself.

If You Have Young Children

Another suggestion in the area of scheduling: When your children are very small, stress the convenience of offering evening and weekend appointments to your clients, in particular, for resume consultations (if this is an area you pursue). Basically, unless you use a form of sitter/child care, evening is the only time when you'll be able to meet with clients uninterrupted if your husband/significant other can care for the kids at the end of the day. This is a big plus for clients, though, and you can market it accordingly. Most office suite services and dedicated resume companies offer appointments *only* during the hours of 9:00 to 5:00. With extended hours your business is more user-friendly. No one needs to know that it's to suit *your* convenience and lifestyle. When scheduling appointments, you need never explain any of your personal reasons for doing business the way in which you do—you can simply state, "Our appointment book is completely filled for the next few days [or week], but I do still have a few evening openings and one appointment left on Saturday."

Appointment Timing

Determining the proper amount of time to allot for an appointment, like many aspects of this business, is an imprecise science. As a minimum you should allow at least fifteen minutes per "appointment," even for a supposedly quick pickup of completed work or drop-off of a project. If a client is picking up a lengthy project and your policy is to allow review/proofreading in your office, take this time into account. For a thirty- or forty-page proposal, an hour might be necessary. Provided that the client does *not* require your active attendance *and* you can work on other projects, you don't charge the client for that time spent in your office (you charge only for the time in which you are actually working with the client on any revisions).

For clients dropping off work, it is typical to allow between five and ten minutes "off the clock" (noncharged time) for the client to briefly review instructions. Any time beyond that should be added to your overall time charge for the project. At the point when you are scheduling an appointment, you should attempt to clarify the purpose of the meeting, nature of the project, and amount of time that may be required to review it.

When you are meeting with resume clientele (if this is a service offering), the time requirements for appointments will vary substantially. For basic typesetting of a resume that the client has already written, no more than five to ten minutes should be necessary (once again, charge for any time after that—or build it into your flat rate); likewise, proofing of a resume you've simply typeset should not take more than five to ten minutes. If a client who has contracted for this level of service begins a dialogue asking your opinion of how something is phrased, beyond a quick response, I would recommend mentioning that you'd be happy to provide consultation services at your appropriate hourly rate (and, if your appointment schedule allows, handling it at that precise point; otherwise, it would need to be scheduled for a different time).

Resume clients for whom you've booked a complete consultation would typically be informed in their initial inquiry telephone call to allow a certain amount of time for the appointment (commonly between one and one and one half hours). If my scheduling permits, I try to keep a two-hour slot open for full resume consultations; if the appointment wraps up in just an hour, I then have the next hour available to at least rough out my thoughts on how to present the client's accomplishments and background information. I find, as a general rule, that the quicker I can work on a creative project after the initial appointment (be it resume development from scratch or creation of a brochure or newsletter), the easier the ideas flow (before my notes get "cold"). My thoughts are fresh, immediately on the heels of the consultation, and I spend much less time trying to recall other points made in the consultation that I may not have written down.

In spite of best efforts to schedule appropriate appointment times, occasionally more than one client will show up at the office at a given time. The client who is within the scheduled appointment time has the priority; depending on the confidentiality of the work, I will advise the second client at the door that he or she is a bit early, and because I am meeting with another client confidentially, I ask if the person would mind waiting a few minutes in his or her car. If the initial client meeting is not confidential, I ask the first client if he or she would object to client #2 waiting in another portion of my office (where there is a sofa); there is usually no objection, and the matter is resolved. If a client is significantly late for an appointment and there is another scheduled to begin very shortly, I advise the late client of this situation and either offer to meet partially at that point, with a reschedule at the earliest available time, or offer to reschedule the entire appointment. I don't allow the second appointment to slip (if that client is on time) just because the first client was tardy. Using diplomacy, tact, and basic consideration, these are easily resolved situations. By the way, I don't charge late clients for the time they were late, nor do I charge for appointments cancelled at the last minute or "no-shows" (relatively infrequent).

If You Have Kids . . . "Tot Techniques"

The following section was created strictly for those with children. Depending on the ages of your kids, some of the following suggestions may prove to be very useful:

- If your kids are old enough, try to "employ" them in your business. Obvious ideas: stuffing and sealing envelopes, applying postage, applying labels, operating the photocopier, collating, filing, and organizing files, cabinets, and bookcases. Pre-teen and teenage "computer whizzes" may be very helpful to you in doing simple typing tasks on the computer (this is ideal if you someday have a second computer system). Even the youngest children can "play office" and help organize drawers of safe contents (keep them away from staplers, correction fluid, rubber cement, sharp scissors, etc.) and "open the mail" (save junk mail in a folder for this).

For older kids who can really perform useful tasks, be sure to pay them for their work on some equitable scale (age-dependent again, maybe 50 cents or $1.00 an hour). For younger children have a good supply of interesting, fun-colored stickers on hand and make up a chart on your computer; award them stickers for jobs well-completed.

- You might consider setting aside a shelf or a drawer in your office filled with child-friendly "work" materials. Here is where the junk mail comes in handy for the younger children. If you order from some of the office supply catalog vendors, you'll soon be receiving lots of extra catalogs. Kids love to go through these looking for things. If you know you're going to be on the phone with a "regular" client (so that a little controlled background "kid" noise is not objectionable), assign your child the project of finding an orange file folder, a red pencil, a bulletin board, and so on in a large office catalog. If the catalog is no longer needed and your children are old enough to have and use rounded, child-safe scissors, you can have them cut out and tape or glue pictures to construction paper.

- With somewhat older children you can "negotiate" time. This works for perhaps the six- to ten-year-old category of kids: "If you will read quietly or work on your puzzle book for the next hour, Mom will be able to spend time with you at the park [going for a walk, going to the library, etc.]."

- In my family we're not TV-watchers, but I do have a small library of *Parent* magazine's "Kidsongs" videotapes and several Disney videotapes that we allow the kids to watch. If you are really under a deadline and cannot watch the movie with your children, you can perhaps plan to be proofreading (if you have excellent concentration) while sitting on the sofa with them while they watch a film. Or perhaps you can arrange to be doing your collating, filing, and the like with them.

- In designing my home office, which was built onto the home specifically for my business, I planned it to be large enough to include an area where we have a library of books, a TV with a VCR (in my business I help clients practice interview techniques through the use of videotapes), a children's plastic picnic/activity table, and a big wraparound sofa to separate that area from my work area. There are hundreds of children's books on the shelves, plus coloring books and crayons, for the use of not only my children but the children of my clients as well. The sofa is useful as a waiting area for those times when two clients are here at the same time (as I mentioned earlier, I never deliberately schedule two clients at the same time, but it happens).

- Child/pet gates are a useful investment, depending on the layout of your home/office. When my children were babies, I used the gates to keep them in my office with me (when they weren't playing in the playpen). As the older two (twins) reached three or four and were playing in their playroom, I'd use a gate to keep one or the other from dashing away from their Dad or babysitter and interrupting me during a client consultation.

  For much older children who can safely be left unattended, a gate is a useful reminder that Mom is working and is to be disturbed only in an emergency (this is particularly helpful if there is not a door to your office, only an open doorway).

- If your office is separated from the rest of your home by a door, installing a message board on the door can make good sense. You can advise family members "Meeting with a Client [or On the Telephone]—Please Do Not Disturb." Simply closing the door can be a reminder to children that you are not to be disturbed. During times of the day when interruptions would be OK, you can establish an "open door policy," that way your family will know it is OK to interrupt.

- Keep a large, attractive toy box in one area of your office (i.e., if your kids are permitted to play in your office) into which you can quickly stow toys prior to opening the door for an early arriving client. Always encourage your kids, from the time they are very young, to pick up their toys and games before getting out something new so that they'll have good, quick cleanup habits.

The Business of Actually Getting the Work Done

This section relates to planning your business schedule and arranging appointments. Based on your own circumstances, time clock, and preferences, you will quickly develop a sense of the best times to work on different types of projects.

As a general guideline, plan to accomplish longer, more involved projects (writing a resume, composing original cover letters, etc.) during "off" office hours and (if you have kids) when your children are sleeping or someone else is caring for them. Your productivity will be greatly enhanced (as will your concentration) if you are not interrupted by the doorbell ringing, the telephone ringing, or your children fighting.

Reserve projects that can be done with many interruptions and less concentration for during the day when you are between appointments or telephone calls and/or the children (if any) are in your office. Projects lending themselves to interruptions might include long typing assignments, thesis typing, and so on. Keep a small clock by your computer/typewriter. *Always* use a Client Production Schedule for each project to log the time on and off the project—this is especially important for times when there are telephone interruptions too.

Be sure to invest in a screen-saver program for your computer monitor (After Dark has a great one). A program with a "message" selection that displays the message you previously entered, "typing" (with the sound of an actual typewriter) it across the screen after a pre-determined lapse of time when no activity has occurred, is very useful. This accomplishes two things: (1) It saves your monitor screen from having the image burned in, and (2) it simulates an "office" sound that is lightly audible over the telephone while you're on a business call and helps to muffle "family" noises. I set my screen saver to begin after one minute of inactivity. My message is one more promotional message (my clients can see the monitor from their seat at the conference table): "Comprehensive Services Plus—Our Business Is Making *You* Look Good!"

As discussed earlier, when you are accepting a client's project, specific instructions should be recorded on a Client Work Order. In addition, all materials should be placed into a manila folder (one hundred can be purchased inexpensively from an office supply warehouse—usually for under $3.00 or $4.00). When a client picks up a project, present the completed work in the same plain manila folder with your label affixed to the front. Use a kraft envelope of the corresponding size for large projects. This is inexpensive and looks professional. If you decide to invest more in your personalized office supplies, you can order custom-printed file folders and envelopes from your printer.

Refer to chapter 5 for information about using the Project Status/Deadline Sheet. This form will allow you to organize and prioritize your work. I recommend preparing a new list at the end of each business day to reorganize projects that have come in through the course of the day that may take precedence over other projects previously recorded. When you begin your work the following morning, you'll have a clear picture of what needs to be accomplished and when.

Your Image and the Image of Your Business

Much has been said and written about the importance of your own image to being successful in business. The "dress for success" mentality certainly permeated the corporate culture during the early 1980s, particularly for women, who were advised to dress for the job they *wanted* to have, not the job they *currently* had.

I have always believed home-based professionals have flexibility with this aspect of their business; however, you are as professional as the demeanor you convey. Even in a home-based situation, it is possible to create a very polished, professional, and businesslike setting and style if you convey absolute authority and confidence in your manner of interacting with your clients. You may want to give consideration to "dressing up" in more conservative business attire for meeting with first-time clients (imperative when you are meeting in their offices). This is a particularly good idea with *business* clientele, as opposed to students or even resume clients; you may feel comfortable in your sweats for most subsequent meetings in your home provided that your *demeanor* is absolutely courteous, polished, and professional.

Much of this will be determined based on your own clientele. I work with a number of health care professionals as well as sales executives—many of whom operate from *their* home offices. They arrive for appointments attired in shorts, jeans, or whatever very casual attire is appropriate for the season. I don't feel a need to "dress to impress" for these meetings. We're all professionals—and on equal ground, regardless of our apparel. Of course, this assumes that while you may be casual, you are not messy—nor are your clothes unclean! Good grooming rules are never put aside.

On the other hand, when I am meeting with someone during a time of day when I know the person is coming directly from his or her office or a business appointment, I will dress more professionally. I believe that allows both of us to be more at ease. First-time resume clients that are professionals are also met with me dressed in more office-appropriate attire. Clients who require (and pay for) a Saturday-night or Sunday-morning appointment, however, might just find me in gardening attire, regardless of who they are and what their business is; it's much the same as going into any corporate office on a Saturday—you won't see any suits, ties, or heels.

As in all other matters related to developing your business, use your own good judgment in determining dress for client meetings.

7

Growing the Business

Managing Business Growth

While you might be tempted to chuckle and inclined to overlook this section, it's probably worthwhile to consider what can happen to your business in terms of growth. Any entrepreneur should possess optimism as a characteristic. Assuming you are an optimist, then, we'll presume your business is going to be successful and grow. To what extent would you like it to expand?

While it is true that limits of growth are, to an extent, only those you place on them, it is important to recognize that *at some point* you will be required to assess the overall future of your business. If you grow at a conservative 10–15 percent per year, it will take you a number of years to "max" out in terms of your ability to handle all of the work of your business. If, on the other hand, you enjoy even faster success (my own has been nearer to 25 or 30 percent per year), you will quickly reach a point when you must make critical decisions. After all, if you do all the work yourself, there are only a certain number of hours available each day (even if you choose to work sixteen or eighteen of them!), a certain number of days per week available (again, even if you choose to work all seven), and so on. What's a successful entrepreneur to do?

Well, one of the obvious things that many first-time business owners neglect to consider is this: Perhaps you are not charging enough for your services. There is a thought in this industry that goes something like this: "If you are getting *no* complaints about your prices whatsoever, you are not charging enough." This is not to give permission to gouge your clients, but it *may* be a good idea, if you find you are working fifty, sixty, or seventy hours a week, week in and week out, to reassess your rates and those of your competition—and then implement a price increase. What's the worst thing that can happen? You may find yourself working fewer hours per week, being happier, and *making more money.* Not a bad result.

Considering Other Profit Centers/Service Offerings

The other thing solid business growth does is permit you the option of specializing on those aspects of the business you particularly enjoy. When most secretarial services begin, they handle any and all work that comes their way. From typing student term papers to doing transcription, they'll "do it all." This is fine, for diversity is interesting, the clientele are unique, and the profits are there. But as your business really hits stride, you may want to rethink your service offerings. Do you really *like* typing student papers? Perhaps you've found, as have a number of people in this business, that term paper typing can be an area fraught with rush deadlines, last-minute (and usually unreasonable) requests, little appreciation, and, unfortunately, occasional bounced checks. Do you need this headache and hassle? Maybe not. Perhaps you decide to stop posting notices at local campus centers. Maybe you take a line off your business cards and from your Yellow Pages advertising that says you type "term papers, theses, and dissertations." The same holds true for any other profit center—even if it's profitable, if you don't really love it, now is the time in your business cycle to truly focus on the services that are profitable *and* that you enjoy.

If writing is your love and you've enjoyed dabbling in newsletter, brochure, and cover letter development, build a specialty around this service offering. It should be billed at a higher rate than basic word processing services, and by cutting out some of the lower-end word processing work (e.g., student typing), you'll have more time to focus on further development of this niche. The bottom line is to evaluate your overall business, assess the projected growth, and make deliberate decisions about areas in which you wish to be positioned.

Is It Time to Get Help?

No, not of the psychological nature, but perhaps what your business needs when you're at a consistently frenzied state of "too much to do, too little time," *is* help—in the form of freelance, subcontracted assistance. By far a better alternative for the sole proprietor who wishes to remain a "small but profitable business," subcontractors, as compared with employees, offer unique advantages for the secretarial service business.

From a tax standpoint, it is necessary to understand the differences between having employees and engaging subcontracted assistance (see related publication of the Internal Revenue Service in Bibliography section of the Appendix or confer with your accounting professional, if you have one). In order for a person to legally fit into a true subcontractor status, he or she must possess his or her own equipment and handle work for you out of his or her own home setting (in other words, not perform the work in your office). In addition, a subcontractor determines when he or she will work (not following a fixed schedule as determined by you). As a practical matter, you can coordinate times suitable to a subcontractor when making the necessary arrangements. A subcontractor, not you, is responsible for ensuring that his or her own tax obligations are met.

A subcontractor arrangement is a good means by which to grow your business without turning work away yet still maintain control over quality and your client relationships (your subcontractors would never meet with your clients, and you would always be checking and proofreading any subcontracted work before presenting it to a client). As with any other form of employee-employer relationship, subcontractor relationships must work well for *you*. Beyond appropriate skills and equipment, there must be a "fit" in terms of working style. You can usually determine fairly quickly in the interview process if the arrangement might be a positive one for you both.

The following forms depict a sample advertisement for seeking qualified subcontractor candidates, an application form, a listing of recommended subject areas to discuss in interviews, a sample typing test, a sample proofreading test, a job sheet for tracking time on projects, individual job sheets, and a sample invoice form for the subcontractor to follow in preparing invoices.

Sample Classified Ad

> **Typist/Word Processor.** Part-time, flexible hours, freelance/subcontractor position. Min. 75 wpm, Mac background, Word 5.1 preferred. Excellent opportunity and pay. Submit resume: P.O. Box 111, Anywhere, USA 88888.

Sample Subcontractor Application

A-1 SERVICES PLUS
P.O. Box 111
ANYWHERE, USA 88888
(888) 888-8888 ☐ FAX (888) 888-8889

Applicant _____ Date _____

Address _____ Telephone _____

Town, State, Zip Code _____

Mailing Address (if Different from Above) _____

Social Security # _____

Equipment/Software Owned_____

Macintosh Experience?	☐ Yes	☐ No
Microsoft Word 5.1 Experience?	☐ Yes	☐ No
Excel 4.0 Experience?	☐ Yes	☐ No
Aldus Pagemaker 5.0 Experience?	☐ Yes	☐ No
Ready-Set-Go Experience?	☐ Yes	☐ No
Quicken Experience?	☐ Yes	☐ No
Dollars + Sense Experience?	☐ Yes	☐ No

Special Skills _____

_____

_____

Typing Speed: wpm _____ errors _____

[Please do not complete this line: tested wpm _____ tested errors _____]

Shorthand Experience? ☐ Yes ☐ No wpm _____

Transcription/Dictaphone Experience? ☐ Yes ☐ No

Medical/Psychological Terminology Background? ☐ Yes ☐ No

Professional Proofreading Experience? ☐ Yes ☐ No

[Do not complete: # errors _____]

**PROFESSIONAL DESKTOP PUBLISHING,
OFFICE, AND EDITORIAL SERVICES**

References

1. Name _____ Relationship _____
   Company _____ Phone # _____
   Address_____

2. Name _____ Relationship _____
   Company _____ Phone # _____
   Address_____

3. Name _____ Relationship _____
   Company _____ Phone # _____
   Address_____

Recent Previous Experience

Employer _____

Address _____

Position Title _____

Employed from _____ to _____

Phone # _____

Employer _____

Address _____

Position Title _____

Employed from _____ to _____

Phone # _____

Desired # Hrs./Week: _____ Max. # Hrs./Week: _____

Availability: Morning (Hours?) _____ Afternoon (Hours?) _____

Evening (Hours?) _____ Weekend (Day/Hrs.?) _____

Any seasonal unavailability (summers off, planned vacation, etc.)_____

_____

Date Available to Begin: _____

Signature of Applicant _____ Date _____

NOT TO BE COMPLETED UNTIL SUBCONTRACTED

In case of emergency, notify: _____

Phone # _____

Date contracted _____ Starting Date _____

Hourly Rate _____
Subcontractor is paid only for hours worked.

A-1 Services Plus will provide subcontractor with Form 1099 in January, to be utilized in completing subcontractor's federal and state income tax forms. A-1 Services Plus will **not** *deduct social security or income tax from subcontractor's payments. Subcontractor is responsible for any and all social security and income tax payments that may be due upon completion of his or her income tax forms. A-1 Services Plus is closed four weeks each calendar year for vacation. Subcontractor understands that all client records, files, and materials are to be maintained and handled in strictest confidence.*

Acknowledged and Received _____
                                                    (Subcontractor Signature)

Date _____

Sample Interview Questionnaire

The following outlines suggested responsibilities to be covered during interviews with candidates for subcontractor positions. The information presented in this example is tailored to my specific business.

Suggested Responsibilities

- word processing (manuscripts, correspondence, cover letters, resumes, presentations)
- typewriting (graduate school applications, employment applications)
- mailings (minutes, newsletters)
- transcription (two-person interviews, one-person dictation)
- courier (depending on time of year and work schedule, may be A.M. and/or afternoon; town[s]; vehicle provided; drive standard?)

Other Key Points

- client confidentiality—*most important factor!* (i.e., resumes—all client contacts handled through this office must be held in strictest confidence)
- noncompete/confidential disclosure agreement
- execute purchase agreement for subcontractor services
- subcontractor to submit weekly summary of hours
- Form 1099 provided
- flexibility in scheduling
- diversity and variety of work
- ideal background: a professional executive secretary with highly polished word processing skills (esp. Mac)

Expectations

- selected candidate will be brought in at an agreed-upon hourly rate
- performance will be evaluated in 4–6 weeks, at which time—based on productivity—an adjustment will be made
- thereafter, performance evaluations will be conducted every 6–9 months, with increases as appropriate based on performance and productivity

IMPORTANT
It is vital that this process work for me in terms of overall productivity.

Interview Notes

Date of Interview _____

Candidate Source _____

Approximate Days Available _____

Approximate Hours Available _____

Weekends? _____

Evenings? _____

Comments: _____

_____

_____

_____

_____

_____

_____

_____

_____

_____

_____

_____

_____

_____

Sample Typing Test

I am interested in seeking the Master's in Health Administration (MHA) for five primary reasons. First, I am very interested in actively working in the health care field and promoting health, prevention, and education.

Second, I have my Bachelor's of Science Degree in Social Work from XYZ University. I believe this degree is a strong asset to blend into the public health field. In the social work program, I developed skills in the areas of networking, advocacy, education, group work, and organizing activities.

Third, I am specifically interested in health care in the areas of drug and alcohol prevention/education, nutrition services, health advocacy, family health services, and gerontology. I feel that one of the greatest strengths of the MHA program is the concept of prevention and education. I am a strong advocate of this innovative philosophy.

Fourth, I have worked for the past four years as a residential counselor in a drug and alcohol treatment center for adolescents. I have seen the pain, anger, and havoc substance abuse has caused adolescents and their families. These clients often do not realize they even have choices as they become more and more immersed in their addiction. I strongly feel that health education, prevention, and promotion will have a positive impact on these social issues.

Fifth, I would value the opportunity to continue to develop my skills and education in the public health field. I am confident that I have the appropriate ability, dedication, and creativity to offer to the MHA program.

Use your computer's word count and clock features to conduct a three-minute timing; allow the applicant time to "warm up" first.

Sample Proofreading Test

December 13 1994

Joan Smith
General Business Copmany
144 Main Street
Anywhere, USA 66666

Dear Joan:

Thank for meeting with me yesterday to to discuss the upcoming regional sale meeting. The purpose or this letter is to outline the plans we made and ot pose some questions. We decided that the overall theme for the meetting wil be "Win with the Best". I will ask The marketing Department to design a logo to be used no all corespondence related to the meeting. The social evening will feature a "Breakout Bash I will coordinate with the hotel to arange decoartions and dance music.

I have come upwith more questions that need answer:

—What is the budget for the social evening?
—Will we provides breakfast before departure?
—Will their be transportation for guests?

Please giv me your response by November 20. I am anxious to implement all of these exciting plans.

Sincerely

Karen Rider

Corrected Proofreading Test

December 13, 1994

Joan Smith
General Business Company
144 Main Street
Anywhere, USA 66666

Dear Joan:

Thank you for meeting with me yesterday to discuss the upcoming regional sales meeting. The purpose of this letter is to outline the plans we made and pose some questions. We decided that the overall theme for the meeting will be "Win with the Best." I will ask the marketing department to design a logo to be used for all correspondence related to the meeting. The social evening will feature a "Breakout Bash." I will coordinate with the hotel to arrange decorations and dance music.

I have come up with more questions which need answers that:

    —What is the budget for the social evening?
    —Will we provide breakfast before departure?
    —Will there be transportation for guests?

Please give me your response by November 20. I am anxious to implement all of these exciting plans.

Sincerely,

Karen Rider

Sample Individual Job Sheet
[use one per client project]

Subcontractor Name _____

Date of Project	Nature of Project (Client Name, Type of Work)	Start Time	End Time	Total Time (In Hours, Minutes)

Copy multiple times.

Sample Subcontractor Job Sheet

Subcontractor Name _____

Date of Project	Nature of Project (Client Name, Type of Work)	Start Time	End Time	Total Time

Sample Subcontractor Invoice Form

Subcontractor Name _____

[address/telephone information]

Invoice for Services Rendered to: Date _____
A-1 Services Plus
P.O. Box 111
Anytown, USA 11111

Date of Project	Nature of Project	# of Hours @ ____/hr.*	Extension

Total Hours: _____ Total Due: _____

Subcontractor Signature _____ Soc. Sec. # _____

For A-1 SERVICES PLUS USE ONLY: Date Paid _____ Check # _____

* Agreed-upon hourly rate

Assessing a Move out of the Home

Because this is a book about establishing and operating a successful home-based secretarial service, I won't devote much space to this topic other than to say it may become a point of consideration in your long-range business planning. As you carefully assess your overall objectives, you may realize that becoming a corporation with a number of employees and having a retail storefront or executive suite location are appealing. You may eventually decide that a separation of your work and your home is important. Still, for many home-based secretarial service operators who have been successfully in business for a number of years, *staying* home-based is a primary objective.

If you are considering moving your business out of your home, be aware of the following points. Beyond the expenses of office overhead and changing your business cards, stationery, and Yellow Pages advertising (as well as any other advertising you do), there will be a commute and its associated costs. You will be tied down to maintaining regular, storefront hours typical of most executive suite or retail space secretarial services. Because you will be "susceptible" to walk-in traffic, you'll need to consider, almost immediately, having at least one employee to serve as receptionist and cover the front of the office when you can't be there (for the entire day, as in illness, or for a half-hour while you have lunch). This brings up immediate concerns about having employees, perhaps providing insurance and benefits and the like, in addition to another salary to support.

For many entrepreneurs starting their own home-based businesses, including secretarial services, a motivating factor was to leave the corporate pressures, the lengthy commute, and a less-than-satisfying environment in exchange for being the boss, setting one's own salary *and* hours, and developing an interesting client base. For those with young children, starting a business often represents an alternative to full-time child care and rarely seeing their children as they grow up.

Considering the explosive growth of home-based professionals in nearly every industry, home-based secretarial service operators are receiving more recognition, respect, and envy than ever before. With the significant technological gains in just the past five years alone, a home office can compete on equal footing with any executive suite or retail setup. Quality is a characteristic, as is professionalism, that can be provided from nearly any office setting, including home-based.

A final point to consider in this evaluation: Do you enjoy the flexibility and advantages available to you in working from your home? Are you willing to give these up and—if so—in exchange for what advantages that executive suite or retail storefront space would offer? Once you've really examined your business objectives and personal goals, you'll be in a good position to assess if a *physical* move is the right move for your business.

Professional and Personal Growth

Establishing and operating a successful home-based secretarial and office support service will bring greater rewards than you can possibly imagine—and in this success you will realize tremendous personal and professional growth. But the learning never stops, and the opportunities for even greater success (however you define this somewhat intangible term) never cease to present themselves. The directions you chart for your business will be a function of your own interests, personal objectives, and desires.

Through membership in professional associations and community organizations, you will have many opportunities to promote your business and your success in establishing and operating it . . . if you so choose. Many owners of secretarial services move into such interesting and lucrative areas as public speaking, teaching, writing, and consulting. The opportunities are truly limitless, grounded only by your own set of objectives and expertise. Good luck, and *enjoy* growing your business!

Appendix

Periodicals/Information

Bootstrappin' Entrepreneur™
c/o Research Done Write!™
Department JLM
8726 South Sepulveda Boulevard
Suite B261
Los Angeles, CA 90045-4082
(310) 568–9861

With excellent money-saving tips on all areas from marketing to promotion and sales for small businesses in general, this quarterly publication features inspirational articles based on the firsthand experiences of others who are successful in their businesses. Send a self-addressed, stamped, #10 business envelope for more information.

Cut & Paste
D.S. Designs
P.O. Box 363
Valley Cottage, NY 10989
(800) 745–4037

Entrepreneur
2392 Morse Avenue
Irvine, CA 92714

Home Office Computing
Scholastic, Inc.
730 Broadway
New York, NY 10003

Home Office Computing is a monthly magazine for home-based business owners with computers; each issue includes excellent marketing and promotional tips, equipment and software reviews, a regular desktop publishing column, and occasional articles related specifically to word processing/typing businesses.

Homeworking Mothers
Department JLM
Mothers' Home Business Network
P.O. Box 423
East Meadow, NY 11554
(516) 997–7394

Homeworking Mothers is a quarterly publication especially focused on home-based business pursuits for mothers with children at home. The publication provides good suggestions and ideas, lots of specific information, and support. Georganne Fiumara, the editor, founded the Mothers' Home Business Network, a national organization with more than 5,000 members, in 1984. A freelance writer and columnist, she has written numerous articles for *Family Circle* regarding mothers who work at home. For a free, four-page brochure, a membership kit, and a sample article, send a self-addressed, stamped, #10 business envelope.

How to Run a Successful Homebased Word Processing/
Desktop Publishing Service: A Resource Package
Nina Feldman Connections
Department JLM
6407 Irwin Court
Oakland, CA 94609
(510) 655–4296

Nina Feldman has been providing home-based word processing/desktop publishing and computer support referral services since 1981. Send a self-addressed, stamped, #10 business envelope to obtain information about the publications and services she provides.

In Business
Magna Publications, Inc.
2718 Dryden Drive
Madison, WI 53704

Keyboard Connection
Department JLM
P.O. Box 338
Glen Carbon, IL 62034
(618) 667–4666; fax (618) 667–8002

Keyboard Connection (*KC*) is an excellent quarterly newsletter chock-full of relevant information to keep the secretarial/office support services owner on the "cutting edge." The editor, Nancy Malvin, has operated her own successful home-based business, Malvin Business and Editing Service, since 1982 and has been publishing *KC* since 1988.

A library of all back issues of *KC* is available, as are individual back issues. In addition, the editor has compiled a complete samples package for start-up secretarial services, including sample business cards, rate sheets, flyers, policy statements, work order, invoice statement, and sales letter. *KC* also conducts surveys periodically and publishes the results in a report for the use of secretarial service owners. The most recent report, *Ethical Standards in the Office Support Industry: A Special Report,* is must-reading on any business support service owner's list.

Send a self-addressed, stamped, #10 business envelope to obtain additional information about a subscription and available publications; send $4.00 for sample issue of *Keyboard Connection.*

> *Qualitype Publications*
> Department JLM
> 5852 Oak Meadow Drive
> Yorba Linda, CA 92686

Lynette Smith has created nearly a dozen relevant guides designed to help entrepreneurs in the office support services profession. Five of her most popular references are noted here; send a self-addressed, stamped, #10 business envelope to obtain a complete listing of materials available.

As a Matter of Policy (item #JM-3, $5.95)
101 Marketing Tips You Can Take to the Bank (item #JM-2, $5.95)
Qualitype Sample Packet (item #JM-6, $4.00)
Profitable Thesis Keyboarding and Copyediting (item #JM-7, $8.95)
How to Give a Good Estimate (item #JM-10, $6.45)

> *S.O.S. (Save Our Sanity) Newsletter*
> Department JLM
> Route 2, Box 340
> Charleston, WV 25314
> (800) 457–1113

Call to obtain a free issue.

S-O-S (Secretarial and Office Support Services) Quarterly
Department JLM
1431 Willow Brook Cove #4
St. Louis, MO 63146
(314) 567-3636

Write for complete information.

Success
Success, Inc.
342 Madison Avenue
New York, NY 10173

Technique
P.O. Box 9164
Hyattsville, MD 20781-9164

The Word Advantage (a quarterly newsletter published by the author of this book, Jan Melnik, of Comprehensive Services Plus)
    For a one-year subscription, send $15 (or $25, for a two-year subscription) to:
    P.O. Box 718
    Department GP
    Durham, CT 06422

Each issue includes
- great ideas for new profit centers
- successful techniques for improving your productivity *and* profitability
- details on how to expand into broader market areas
- pricing Q & A
- sample ads, brochure copy, promotional tips
- plus a forum for subscribers to exchange good ideas and tips for running a home-based business and managing the challenges of simultaneously raising young children.
- Also available from Jan Melnik is a comprehensive guide (120 pages) entitled *How to Operate a Successful, Home-based Resume Service.* A perfect add-on profit center to a secretarial service, this book provides complete details for attracting clients, conducting effective consulta-

tions, writing distinctive resumes, crafting cover letters that get results, booking repeat business, and establishing yourself as an expert in this field. To order ($19.85, ppd., payable to CSP) or to obtain further information, write to P.O. Box 718, Department GP, Durham, CT 06422.

Professional Associations/Assistance

The National Association of Secretarial Services (NASS)
3637 Fourth Street North
Suite 330
St. Petersburg, FL 33704
(813) 823–3646

Call for both information about the national organization and details about the local/regional chapter nearest you.

SCORE (Service Corps of Retired Executives)
c/o Small Business Development Center Headquarters
1129 Twentieth Street, NW, #410
Washington, DC 20036

Contact your local SCORE chapter to arrange for a complimentary small business consultation.

Independent Sales Organizations (to obtain merchant account)

Bankcard $olutions
140 Thompson Street, #26E
East Haven, CT 06513
(800) 260–1500; (203) 466–1500

Cardservice International
21122 Erwin Street
Woodland Hills, CA 91367
(800) 593–3500

Security Merchant Service
404 Dakota Trail
Irving, TX 75063
(214) 401–1437

Teleflora CreditLine
Attn. Credit Card Operation
12233 West Olympic Boulevard
Los Angeles, CA 90064
(800) 325–4849; (310) 826–5233, ext. 4000

Office Supply Vendors

Mail Order

". . . because It's Your Business"™
Artistic Greetings
P.O. Box 91
Elmira, NY 14902-1623
(800) 933–4648

BeaverPrints™
Main Street
Bellwood, PA 16617
(800) 847–7237

Paper Access
23 West 18th Street
New York, NY 10011
(800) PAPER 01 (727–3701)

Paper Direct
205 Chubb Avenue
Lyndhurst, NJ 07071
(800) A•PAPERS (272–7377)

Penny Wise Office Products
(offers discount to subscribers of *Homeworking Mothers*)
4350 Kenilworth Avenue
Edmonston, MD 20781
(800) 942–3311

Queblo
1000 Florida Avenue
Hagerstown, MD 21741
(800) 523–9080

Quill Corporation
P.O. Box 1450
Lebanon, PA 17042-1450
(717) 272–6100

Reliable
1001 W. Van Buren Street
Chicago, IL 60607
(800) 735–4000

Streamliners
5 Pleasant View Drive
P.O. Box 480
Mechanicsburg, PA 17055
(800) 544–5779

Viking Office Products
13809 South Figueroa Street
P.O. Box 61144
Los Angeles, CA 90061
(800) 421–1222

Wholesale Supply Company
P.O. Box 23437
Nashville, TN 37202
(800) 962–9162

Time Management/Scheduling Aids

DayTimers, Inc., One DayTimer Plaza, Allentown, PA 18195-1551;
(215) 395–5884. *Calendars and time planners.*

Franklin International Institute, Inc., P.O. Box 25127, Salt Lake City, UT
84125-0127; (800) 654–1776. *Calendars and time planners.*

Bibliography

Atkinson, William. *Working at Home: Is It For You?* Dow Jones–Irwin, 1985.

Belkin, Gary S. *How to Start and Run Your Own Word Processing Business.* John Wiley & Sons, 1984.

Blake, Gary. *How to Promote Your Own Business.* New American Library, 1983.

Brabec, Barbara. *Homemade Money: The Definitive Guide to Success in a Home Business.* Betterway Publications, 1989.

Bradley, Marianne T. *How to Start a Successful Home-based Word Processing Business.* Vesper Publishing.

Branson, John J. *How to Start a Word Processing Business at Home.* Prentice Hall, 1985.

Brenner, Robert C. *Pricing Guide for Desktop Publishing Services.* Vesper Publishing.

The Chicago Manual of Style. University of Chicago Press, 1993 (14th ed.).

Cook, Mel. *Home Business, Big Business: How to Launch Your Home Business and Make It a Success.* Collier Books, Macmillan Publishing Co., 1992.

Cornish, Clive G. *Basic Accounting for the Small Business.* TAB Books, 1988.

Davenport, Lynne. *Home Transcribing: Could You? Should You? A Practical Guide to Establishing a Professional Transcribing Service at Home.* Dalyn Press, 1984.

Dean, Sandra Linville. *How to Advertise: A Handbook for Small Business.* Enterprise Publications, 1980.

Drouillard, Anne. *How to Earn $25,000 a Year or More Typing at Home.* F. Fell, 1973.

Edwards, Paul and Sarah. *Working From Home.* Jeremy Tarcher, Inc., 1990 (3rd ed.).

Edwards, Paul and Sarah, and Douglas, Laura Clampitt. *Getting Business to Come to You.* Jeremy Tarcher, Inc. 1991.

Entrepreneur Magazine's Complete Guide to Owning a Home-based Business. Bantam Books, 1990.

Ferner, Jack. *Successful Time Management: A Self-teaching Guide.* John Wiley & Sons, 1980.

Fox, Frank. *Starting a Successful Secretarial Service.* The National Association of Secretarial Services (3637 Fourth Street North, Suite 330, St. Petersburg, FL 33704), 1988.

Glenn, Peggy. *How to Start and Run a Successful Home Typing Business.* Pigi Publications, 1983.

Glenn, Peggy. *Word Processing Profits at Home: A Complete Business Plan for the Self-employed Word Crafter.* Aames-Allen Publishing, 1987.

Gray, Ernest A. *Profitable Methods for Small Business Advertising.* John Wiley & Sons, 1984.

Hodson, Marcia. *Word Processing Plus: Profiles of Home-based Success.* CountrySide Business Publications, 1991.

Holtz, Herman. *How to Start and Run a Writing and Editing Business.* John Wiley & Sons, 1992.

Internal Revenue Service:

Publications

Basis of Assets (#551)

Business Use of a Car (#917)

Business Use of Your Home (#587)

Depreciation (#534)

Determining Whether a Worker Is an Employee (#SS-8)

Index to Tax Publications (#900)

Miscellaneous Deductions (#529)

Recordkeeping for a Small Business (#552, #583)

Sales and Other Dispositions of Assets (#544)

Self-Employment Tax (#533)

Taxable and Nontaxable Income (#525)

Tax Guide for Small Business (#334)

Tax Information for Direct Sellers (#911)

Taxpayers Starting a Business (#583)

Tax Withholding and Declaration of Estimated Tax (#505)

Travel, Entertainment, and Gift Expenses (#463)

Forms

1040 (U.S. Individual Income Tax Return)
1040-ES (Estimated Tax for Individuals)
4562 (Depreciation and Amortization)
8829 (Expenses for Business Use of Your Home)

Schedules

A (Itemized Deductions)
B (Interest and Dividend Income)
C (Profit or Loss from Business)
D (Capital Gains and Losses)
SE (Self-Employment Tax)

To request information, write Internal Revenue Service, 1111 Constitution Avenue, NW, Washington, DC 20224.

Kozlow, Stephen G. *How to Start Your Own Secretarial Services Business at Home.* SK Publications, 1980.

Loftus, Michele. *How to Start and Operate a Home-based Word Processing or Desktop Publishing Business.* Bob Adams, Inc. Publishers, 1990.

Lonngren, Betty. *Starting Your Own Secretarial Business: Getting Clients, Selecting Equipment.* Contemporary Books, 1982.

Luscher, Keith F. *Advertise! An Assessment of Fundamentals for Small Business.* K&L Publications, 1991.

Morgenstern, Steve. *No-Sweat Desktop Publishing.* AMACOM, 1992.

Mullins, Carolyn J. *The Complete Manuscript Preparation Style Guide.* Prentice-Hall, 1982.

Murray, Jean Wilson. *Starting and Operating a Word Processing Service.* Pilot Industries, 1983.

Parker, Yana. *Resume Pro: The Professional's Guide.* Ten Speed Press, 1993.

Semon, Larry. *"Did You See My Ad?": When, Why, and How to Advertise the Small Business.* Brick House Publishing Co., 1988.

Shenson, Howard L. *The Contract and Fee Setting Guide for Consultants and Professionals.* John Wiley & Sons, 1990.

Small Business Administration—various publications, including

The ABC's of Borrowing (#FM 1)
Advertising (#MT 11)
Basic Budgets for Profit Planning (#FM 3)

Budgeting in a Small Service Firm (#1.015)
The Business Plan for Homebased Business (#MP 15)
Business Plan for Small Service Firms (#MP 11)
Checklist for Going into Business (#MP 12)
Credit and Collections (#MA 1.007)
Effective Business Communications (#MP 1)
Financial Management: How to Make a Go of Your Business (#111W)
Insurance Checklist for Small Business (#MA2.018)
Marketing for Small Business: An Overview (#MT 2)
Planning and Goal Setting for Small Business (#2.010)
Pricing Your Products and Services Profitably (#FM 13)
Recordkeeping in a Small Business (#FM 10)
Selecting the Legal Structure for Your Business (#MA 6.004)
Should You Lease or Buy Equipment? (#MP 8)
Understanding Cash Flow (#FM 4)

To request free order forms, as well as a directory of all titles available, write Small Business Administration, P.O. Box 15434, Ft. Worth, TX 76119.

Smith, Lynette M. *How to Start a Word Processing Business at Home.* Qualitype, 1992.

Temple, Mary. *How to Start a Secretarial and Business Service.* Pilot Books, 1978.

Turabian, Kate L. *A Manual for Writers of Term Papers, Theses, and Dissertations.* University of Chicago Press, 1987 (5th ed.).

Vickman, Thomas, *Home-Office Tax Deductions.* Enterprise Publishing, 1988.

Vrooman, Alan H. *Good Writing: An Informal Manual of Style.* Phillips Exeter Academy Press Book, 1972.

Wallace, Carol Wilkie. *Great Ad! Low-Cost Do-It-Yourself Advertising for Your Small Business.* Liberty Hall Press, 1990.

Waymon, Lynn. *Starting and Managing a Business from Your Home.* U.S. Small Business Administration, Starting and Managing Series, Vol. 2, 1986.

Wilbanks, Patricia M. *How to Start a Typing Service in Your Own Home.* Arco, 1972.

Will, Mimi and Weber, Nancy. *How to Create a Successful Word Processing Business.* PPW Publishing Co., 1983.

Witcher, William K. *How to Solve Your Small Business Advertising Problems.* Advertising Planners, Inc., 1986.

Index

About the Author

Jan Melnik, of Durham, Connecticut, has operated a successful home-based business since 1983. Initially naming the business Professional Services Plus when it was started in Connecticut, she renamed it Comprehensive Services Plus (for better alphabetical placement in the Yellow Pages) upon her relocation to the Boston, Massachusetts, area in 1986. The name Comprehensive Services Plus (CSP) stayed when her family moved back to Connecticut in 1988. A graduate of Bay Path College, Ms. Melnik acquired more than twelve years of professional experience with Fortune 50 corporations prior to starting her own company. She is a contributing writer to *Keyboard Connection* and *Bootstrappin' Entrepreneur* and recently addressed an annual regional NASS conference. She is married to Ron Melnik and is the mother of identical twins, Daniel and Weston (born in 1987), and Stephen (born in 1990). When she isn't working or mothering, her other passions in life are reading, gardening, and writing children's stories.

Final Thoughts

Salute to Small Business

Once in awhile there's a feeling
Over something you've done right.
And the drive home is different that day.
It feels good and it lasts all night.

It's the difference between the money,
And the time you put in.
You've stopped working for somebody else
Now you're doing it for yourself.

You try to fit into the system,
No more making waves.
You fill out the forms,
Wait for the answers,
But you're numb at the end of the day.

You get tired of seeing all the good ideas
Lost inside the machine,
And you dream of a place,
Where decisions are made,
Because it feels right and that's all that you need.

You've stopped working for somebody else
Now you're doing it for yourself.

—AUTHOR UNKNOWN (extracted from workshop materials presented at Small Business Administration/Southern New England Telephone Company "Success '91 Symposium")

The best advice of all? If you have motivation and energy
and a determination to succeed, then *go for it!*

OTHER TITLES IN GLOBE PEQUOT'S
Home-based Business Series

How to Open and Operate a Bed & Breakfast Home
Third Edition
by Jan Stankus - $14.95

How to Open and Operate a Home-based Catering Business
by Denise Vivaldo - $14.95

How to Open and Operate a Home-based Landscaping Business
by Owen E. Dell - $14.95

How to Open and Operate a Home-based Photography Business
by Kenn Oberrecht - $14.95

How to Open and Operate a Home-based Writing Business
by Lucy V. Parker - $14.95

To order any of these titles with MASTERCARD or VISA, call toll free 1–800–243–0495; in Connecticut call 1–800–962–0973. Globe Pequot offers free shipping on orders of three or more books. There will be a $3.00 shipping charge per book when only one or two books are ordered. Connecticut residents add sales tax.

Please request a complimentary copy of Globe Pequot's book catalogue. We publish quality books on recreation, travel, nature, business, gardening, cooking, crafts, and more.

Prices and availability subject to change.